D0078422

China Among
the Nations of the Pacific

Also of Interest

† *China Briefing, 1981*, edited by Robert B. Oxnam and Richard C. Bush

† *China Briefing, 1980*, edited by Robert B. Oxnam and Richard C. Bush

Technology, Defense, and External Relations in China, 1975–1978, Harry G. Gelber

Southeast Asia and China: The End of Containment, Edwin W. Martin

Military Power and Policy in Asian States: China, India, Japan, edited by Onkar Marwah and Jonathan D. Pollack

Perspectives on a Changing China: Essays in Honor of Professor C. Martin Wilbur, edited by Joshua A. Fogel and William T. Rowe

China's Quest for Independence: Policy Evolution in the 1970s, edited by Thomas Fingar and the *Stanford Journal of International Studies*

Chinese Foreign Policy After the Cultural Revolution, 1966–1977, Robert G. Sutter

† *China, the Soviet Union, and the West: Strategic and Political Dimensions for the 1980s*, edited by Douglas T. Stuart and William T. Tow

† *China: A Political History, 1917–1980* (fully revised and updated), Richard C. Thornton

The People's Republic of China: A Handbook, edited by Harold C. Hinton

† *China's Four Modernizations: The New Technological Revolution*, edited by Richard Baum

† *China's Economic Development: Growth and Structural Change*, Chu-yuan Cheng

Critical Energy Issues in the Asia Pacific Region: The Next Twenty Years, edited by Fereidun Fesharaki

† Available in hardcover and paperback.

Westview Special Studies on China and East Asia

China Among the Nations of the Pacific
edited by Harrison Brown

with a Foreword by J. William Fulbright

The nations that border the Pacific Ocean are becoming increasingly interdependent, and trade among them – a major cohesive force – has already reached substantial proportions. *China Among the Nations of the Pacific* examines this new order, focusing on events in China and on how the PRC will affect and interact with its Pacific neighbors as it looks outward from its former isolation.

The authors – all recognized authorities – address such fundamental issues as China's economy, demographics, food and energy supplies, and relations with the rest of Asia. Will China become a major exporter of energy? Will it remain a major importer of food? Is China destined to become one of Japan's major suppliers of raw materials? Can China resolve its maritime jurisdiction disputes with neighboring countries? How will the perceptions of the nations of Southeast Asia concerning China and the Chinese influence the future course of events? The discussion of these and other questions adds a new dimension to the study of China's external relations.

Harrison Brown is director of the Resource Systems Institute, East-West Center, Honolulu.

This book resulted from a symposium that was organized to celebrate the twentieth anniversary of the founding of the East-West Center in May 1960. The symposium was held at the National Academy of Sciences in Washington, D.C. The distinguished participants had all been directly affiliated with the East-West Center at one time or another. The audience included China scholars, diplomats from the nations of the Asia-Pacific region, members of Congress and their staffs, representatives of U.S. government agencies, and East-West Center alumni.

China Among
the Nations of the Pacific

edited by Harrison Brown

with a Foreword by J. William Fulbright

Westview Press / Boulder, Colorado

337.51
C5392

Westview Special Studies on China and East Asia

All rights reserved. No part of this publication may be reproduced or transmitted in any form or by any means, electronic or mechanical, including photocopy, recording, or any information storage and retrieval system, without permission in writing from the publisher.

Copyright © 1982 by the East-West Center

Published in 1982 in the United States of America by
  Westview Press, Inc.
  5500 Central Avenue
  Boulder, Colorado 80301
  Frederick A. Praeger, Publisher

Library of Congress Cataloging in Publication Data
Main entry under title:
China among the nations of the Pacific.
  (Westview special studies on China and East Asia)
  Papers from a symposium held May 19, 1980 at the National Academy of Sciences, Washington, D.C.
  Includes index.
  1. China—Economic conditions—1976—   —Addresses, essays, lectures. 2. China—Economic policy—Addresses, essays, lectures. 3. China—Foreign economic relations—Addresses, essays, lectures. 4. China—Foreign relations—Addresses, essays, lectures. I. Brown, Harrison Scott, 1917-   . II. Series.
  HC427.92.C463   337.5109   81-14828
  ISBN 0-86531-260-5   AACR2
  ISBN 0-86531-279-6 (pbk.)

m·R
Printed and bound in the United States of America

[1 30 44]

Contents

Foreword, *J. William Fulbright* viii
Preface, *Harrison Brown* xi
Map of China...xii

1. The Chinese Economy in the 1980s,
   Dwight H. Perkins 1

2. China's New Social Fabric: Views of Inside from Outside,
   Godwin C. Chu and Francis L. K. Hsu 15

3. The Great Triangle: China, the U.S.S.R., and Japan,
   Allen S. Whiting 47

4. China's Food Prospects and Import Needs,
   A. Doak Barnett...59

5. China's Population in Perspective,
   Chi-hsien Tuan 69

6. China's Role in the Energy Development of Asia and the
   Pacific: The Next Twenty Years,
   Kim Woodard..85

7. China's Maritime Jurisdictions: The Future of Offshore Oil
   and Fishing
   Choon-ho Park 105

8. Southeast Asia Looks at China,
   Guy J. Pauker...115

The Contributors...127
Index 129

University Libraries
Carnegie Mellon University
Pittsburgh, Pennsylvania 15213

Foreword

J. William Fulbright

I am pleased on this, the twentieth anniversary of the founding of the East-West Center, to be honorary chairman of the symposium "China and the Nations of the Pacific." Twenty years ago, as a member of the United States Senate, I voted for the creation of this unique institution. As early as 1945, I had become interested in trying to promote better relations within the jungle of nations through educational exchanges and helped to develop a program of bilateral exchanges between the United States and other countries. That program, still functioning under the International Communications Agency, in its own way complements the activities of the East-West Center.

Traditional diplomacy's lack of progress in creating a more cooperative spirit among nations suggests most urgently that additional efforts must be put into exchange programs and institutions like the East-West Center if we are ever to resolve the differences among nations in a peaceable manner. As nations become more interdependent and as the major problems confronting them become increasingly difficult to solve, we must all change our attitudes toward the world community. We must change, not only to avoid a fatal nuclear conflict, but also to cope with such problems as pollution of the air and oceans, hunger and malnutrition, overpopulation and underproduction, and depletion of the sources of many raw materials, especially those of energy.

Transnational education, exemplified by the programs of the East-West Center, is the best approach developed thus far to change attitudes toward people with different ethnic, cultural, and ideological characteristics. Differences of language, religion, and customs are truly formidable barriers to understanding and to the development of empathy, but we must surmount them. That is the true mission of this center.

The late Albert Einstein said, after the first nuclear bomb was dropped on Japan, that we must find a new manner of thinking – if we do not, man will be faced with an incalculable catastrophe. This, it seems to me, is the central problem. Can we control the mindless military competition among the major powers and change it into a cooperative contest that will eventually persuade people to accept reason rather than violence as the ultimate means for the reconciliation of differences?

This question was emphasized by two strikingly different articles that appeared in the same recent edition of the *Washington Post*. The first reported that the Committee on the Present Danger, composed of some of the most influential and powerful men in our country, is urging our government to increase our military appropriation by $260 billion over the next six years. This would be in addition to the $130 billion already proposed by the White House. The second article reported that the Soviet Union is now providing all high school students with extensive superenriched training in mathematics and science. The program is reported to be so successful that the U.S. high school system has been rendered primitive by comparison. In short, it is a concerted drive to produce mass education of unmatched quality.

The juxtaposition of these two articles is noteworthy. What a fine thing it would be if we could shift our competition with the Soviets from the arms race to a contest to see which nation can develop the best quality of education. How bright our future would be if each year a committee of experts measured the excellence of the intellect of the high school students of these two countries and decided which were the best educated in various fields.

Comparing this Soviet effort with the report of the Committee on the Present Danger provides an important lesson and a challenge. If we Americans respond properly, the future holds great promise. If we do not respond properly and continue to emphasize only the arms race, we will get only what we deserve – an incalculable catastrophe.

If any lesson can be learned from history, it is that doctrines and causes which arouse men to passion and violence are transitory, that they fade into irrelevance and obsolescence. Only a few years ago, Americans generally regarded China as part of an evil conspiracy, and the Chinese regarded the United States as a dangerous imperialist power. Today, however, we are exploring ways to cooperate for our mutual benefit. Such changes are encouraging and hopeful, but to give them real substance and significance for the future, we must buttress them with educational experience such as that offered by the East-West Center.

Finally, on this twentieth anniversary of the creation of the East-West Center, I want to pay tribute to three people. The late Governor John A. Burns of Hawaii and the late President Lyndon B. Johnson, then the majority leader of the U.S. Senate, played key roles in the creation of this institution. Indeed, had they not persevered, the East-West Center might not have been created at all. Finally, I am pleased to express my appreciation publicly to President Everett Kleinjans for the great service he has given to the Center for so many years. It is a very difficult task to create out of whole cloth a new educational institution, especially a unique one. He has done his job well, and his successful efforts make it possible for all of us to look forward to at least another twenty years of intercultural education and research undertaken at the East-West Center.

NA

Preface

On May 14, 1960, the East-West Center was officially created by the Congress of the United States. As a part of the celebration of the twentieth anniversary of this event, a symposium was held on May 19, 1980, at the National Academy of Sciences in Washington, D.C. The subject "China and the Nations of the Pacific" was selected because the theme for the anniversary year of the East-West Center had been established as "Building a Pacific Community." Clearly, any serious discussion of the possibility of developing a Pacific community organization must include the People's Republic of China as a major factor.

In recent years, the developing countries in the Pacific Basin have been among the fastest-growing countries in the world. A striking characteristic of this growth has been the rapid expansion of international trade in the region. For most of these countries, the growth of exports has averaged more than 20 percent per year. The more developed countries of the region have grown less rapidly; even so, they have done better than the industrial nations of Europe in sustaining real growth.

It has been suggested that international mechanisms for coming to grips with such interdependencies in the Pacific region as trade, investment, food, energy, and mineral commodities are inadequate. In response to such suggestions, hearings have been held in both houses of the Congress of the United States on the idea of a Pacific community. This symposium was organized as part of that general discussion. We hope that the papers presented here will further stimulate thought and debate on the problems of the Pacific region.

— Harrison Brown
Director
Resource Systems Institute, The East-West Center

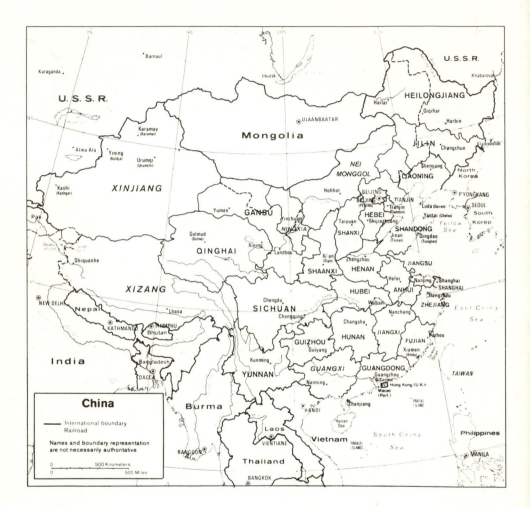

Source: U.S., Department of State, "Background Notes: China," March 1980. [The dotted line denotes the July 1, 1979, expansion of Inner Mongolia (Nei Monggol), whereby the autonomous region received the western portions of Heilongjiang and Jilin provinces, and the northern portions of Liaoning and Gansu provinces and of the Ningxia Hui Autonomous Region. This change restored the borders existing before July 1969.]

1214
China

1
The Chinese Economy in the 1980s

Dwight H. Perkins

For the past three decades, East Asia, not Europe or North America, has been the most rapidly developing part of the world's economy. For a decade or more, Japan has been recognized as an industrial giant. More recently, South Korea, Taiwan, Hong Kong, and Singapore have been duplicating Japan's performance.

Less obvious has been the somewhat more gradual industrialization of the People's Republic of China. A vast rural hinterland, which even in 1980 contained three-quarters or more of China's population, often left visitors with the impression that China's economy had not changed all that much since the 1949 revolution. Where before there were individual family farms, now there were communes; but China was still a land of rice paddies in the south and fields of wheat and millet in the north. In large cities like Shanghai, the poor no longer died in the streets, but the Shanghai Bund looked much the same as it had in the 1930s. The Chinese government's decision not to publish economic statistics further reinforced this image: The failure to make industrial and gross-national-product (GNP) growth rates public presumably indicated that there was little progress to report. China was a land where left and right were locked in battle over which political philosophy would set China's future course. Would China be a genuinely classless and egalitarian society, or would it be an Asian version of the Soviet Union complete with a new political and technocratic elite?

Obscured by the smoke of politics and the closed nature of Chinese society, a fundamental transformation of China's economy was beginning. Even before 1949, industry in the coastal cities had grown. After the revolution, industry spurted ahead in the 1950s, came to a crashing halt when the Great Leap Forward failed and the Soviet Union removed technical support in 1960, but then recovered and surged ahead once again. Further disruption during the Cultural

Revolution hurt, but still the average growth rate from the late 1950s
to the late 1970s was 9 percent a year. By 1980, China's industrial base
was eight times the size reached in the mid-1950s. Steel output was
34.5 million metric tons and electric power generation had reached
282 billion kilowatt hours. In absolute terms, Chinese industry in
1980 was equivalent in size to that of Japan in the early to mid-1960s.
In per capita terms, China had only a small fraction of Japan's industrial capacity, but a base had been created on which further expansion could take place.

There are those who talk and make policy as if China were going to
remain far behind Japan and even farther behind the United States
and the Soviet Union well into the twenty-first century. Those who
think this way do not see the implications of high industrial and gross-
national-product growth rates compounded over the next two or three
decades. A few simple calculations will illustrate the main point.

The 9 percent growth rate achieved by Chinese industry over the
past quarter century led to more than an eightfold rise in industrial
output. Chinese GNP over this same period rose at a rate a bit below 5
percent a year—overall a nearly threefold increase over the past
quarter century. These growth rates were achieved despite the
massive political upheavals and economic policy mistakes that
characterized the period. For the moment, at least, China appears to
have put such upheavals aside. Under these new circumstances, it is
reasonable to think that China's industrial and gross-national-product
growth rates will accelerate. If GNP should rise by 7 percent a year, a
rate still well below the sustained performances of Japan and South
Korea, by the year 2000 the Chinese GNP would be nearly four times
what it is today. If industrial growth should modestly accelerate to a
rate of 10 percent per year, total industrial output would be eight
times what it was in 1980. Put differently, China by the year 2000
would have a GNP and an industrial base substantially larger than
that of Japan in 1980, at least in absolute terms. In per capita terms,
China would be well behind Japan, but there, too, the per capita gap
would be closing.

From the viewpoint of people concerned with the standard of living
of the Chinese people, it is the per capita growth rates that matter. For
those concerned with the world balance of power, however, the absolute figures are important. If China achieves the kind of growth projected here, within two decades the nation's GNP will pass the US
$1,000 billion mark (in 1980 dollars). A future Chinese government
willing to maintain current levels of defense spending would have a
military budget of around US $70 to 90 billion, a formidable figure but

still well below what could be achieved if the perceived external threats were great enough.

Military power is more than a large budget, of course. Large numbers of tanks and aircraft are of limited use if most of these weapons are obsolete. China today, for example, could expand its defense budget far beyond current levels, but what would it do with another 1,000 MIG-19s? The question for the year 2000 is whether this gap between China's current level of technology and those of the major powers will close along with the GNP gap. No one really knows the answer. Still, the past century has seen one nation after another catch up with the world leader's level of technology. "Follower" nations do not have to repeat all the mistakes or travel down all the blind alleys of those at the forefront of technological advance. Thus, there is no reason to think that the present gap between the level of technology in China and that in the United States or the Soviet Union will last for long. The Chinese are presently making an all-out effort to catch up. Therefore, is it still plausible to think that China cannot do what the Soviet Union and Japan did in the decades immediately after World War II?

China, by virtue of its enormous population and rich cultural heritage, has always been one of the world's great nations. Political unification and genuine independence from foreign control after 1949 turned China into a significant power, but one that could not exercise its power very far beyond its borders. Economic development over the next two decades could complete the task of putting China's power nearly on a par with that of the Soviet Union and the United States.

If China is to become a major world power over the next two decades and not just an Asian power, U.S. and other policies toward China should be based on that prospect. To talk about playing the "China card" against the Soviet Union, as if China were in the same league as bases in Somalia or the MX missile, is to miss the significance of what has been happening over the past two decades and, even more, what may happen over the next two decades. Similarly, to oppose efforts by the United States to build closer relations with China because such steps upset the Soviet Union is also to miss the point. If growth in China continues, China itself will have a position of power within the world roughly comparable to that of the U.S.S.R. Full comparability might not exist within two decades but will come soon enough thereafter that current U.S. policy toward China should be based on that expectation. If we wait until China has reached superpower status, it may be too late to build a relationship different from what we now have with the Soviet Union.

The underlying theme of this chapter is that because of rapid growth to date and even more rapid expected future growth, policy toward China should be one of the cornerstones of U.S. international relations, not a building block toward some other, more fundamental goal. But will this rapid growth in fact occur? If it does not, then the cost of postponing dealing with aspects of United States–China relations will be much less. The next section of this chapter, therefore, is devoted to an analysis of the prospects for sustained economic development in the People's Republic.

Even if development does occur, will Chinese policies continue in the direction of opening up toward the outside world or will China once again turn inward? With its 600-year history of looking inward (since the early Ming dynasty), it would be foolish to be overly optimistic about a permanent Chinese turn outward, but the success or failure of China's current internationally oriented economic policies will have more than a little influence on the ultimate outcome. Thus, economic issues will play a key role in determining China's future world position through a number of different channels.

The Prospects for Growth

How likely is China to achieve sustained economic development? Could the efforts of the late 1970s and early 1980s come to naught? Some have interpreted the "readjustment" in economic policy in 1979 as a sign that severe problems for China's economy lay just ahead and only modest growth could be expected.

The greatest uncertainty about China's economic future lies in the realm of politics. China has had spurts of rapid growth in the past, but these were followed by massive disruptions, such as the Great Leap Forward and the Cultural Revolution. Perhaps periodic upheavals are inherent in governing a country of such great size in accordance with China's authoritarian traditions. Deng Xiaoping, not a young man, is already planning for his successor. Mao Zedong and Zhou Enlai also tried to influence the succession, with results that can hardly be encouraging to Deng.

For all the uncertainty surrounding China's economic future, however, there are reasons for thinking that many aspects of China's current development strategy will outlast Deng Xiaoping's personal rule. To begin with, Deng has moved much more systematically than his predecessor to ensure the kind of succession he desires. Zhao Ziyang and Hu Yaobang have been moved into strategic positions of power. With one exception, Deng's potential opposition on the Politburo has been removed. More important, no one with Mao's stature is likely to appear. A revolution has only one founder; no one else by personal effort can go against the apparatus of the Chinese Communist Party and turn the nation upside down in the process. Leaders will come and go, but in the future their power will be based on coalitions of Party and military leaders.

Could these coalitions swing from one extreme of policy to another as readily as when Mao personally was the main impetus behind such swings? Widespread disillusionment with the Cultural Revolution among China's urban elite would seem to make a return to the policies of the late 1960s difficult. Party leaders were imprisoned and tortured; intellectuals of all stripes were shipped off to the countryside or worse. Few urban youth found jobs in the cities. Most were sent off to the distant northwest or to the remoter regions of the northeast. Factory managers were not allowed to manage; engineers and scientists were constantly interfered with by political activists who asserted their right to decide purely technical matters.

There was a more positive side to the Cultural Revolution, particularly in the rural areas, and many people not purged joined the Party and rose to positions of influence during this period. But one is hard pressed to find people with positive things to say about the 1966–1976 period, and the tales of hardship that one hears today come out in more credible ways than did the rote political phrases of the earlier period. There is now no obvious base of power from which a return to the extreme-left policies of the Cultural Revolution could be launched.

Although it is difficult to see any return soon to policies designed to carry out some of Mao's more utopian visions, it is not at all difficult to envision a turn away from some of the efforts that have characterized the late 1970s and early 1980s. Chinese economic policies in recent times have been consciously influenced by the successes of Japan and even South Korea and Taiwan. The policies pursued have included joint ventures, expanded production for foreign markets, promotion of Western tourism, and membership in the International Monetary Fund (IMF) and the World Bank. Hotels jammed with foreign tourists and businessmen are good for China's foreign exchange position, but the reaction of many individual Chinese has been negative. If the policies work and bring prosperity and greater power to China, they will be tolerated and in time may even be taken for granted. If the policies fail or simply do not live up to expectations, their unpopularity could become the lever used by groups within the Chinese Communist Party to bring down those who advocated opening up China to the outside world in the first place. There is no large constituency in China for the view that turning outward is good in itself. Such a fundamental change must be supported by results.

Will the turn outward bring positive results, that is, will economic performance be substantially better than what would have occurred in the absence of a turn outward? The answer depends most of all on what happens to Chinese exports, a subject to which I shall return later. If the outward turn is successful, that alone will help stabilize Chinese politics. If the policies are perceived as failures, then Chinese politics will be less stable and that instability will contribute further to the failure of the economic policies that were the source of instability in the first place. Foreigners, who are businessmen, after all, prefer to deal with stable regimes and tend to cut back on investment and long-term loans when stability is threatened. Political stability thus depends in part on rapid growth, and rapid growth in turn depends on political stability. Although the prospects for stability are much better than at any time since the 1950s, political in-fighting severe enough to disrupt the economy could still occur. If there is instability, however, growth will not come to a halt but will continue the start-and-stop pattern of the past two decades.

Economic Constraints on Rapid Growth

If one puts aside political issues with all their uncertainty, are there more purely economic or technical barriers to rapid growth? In late 1978 and early 1979, Chinese planners realized that their efforts immediately after the fall of the Gang of Four had been overambitious, and in mid-1979, they announced new, more modest targets. Current goals suggest that China's leaders think they will have trouble achieving even a 6 percent annual increase in gross national product in the early 1980s. Does it follow, then, that there is little hope of China's achieving a 7 percent or higher GNP growth rate? The Chinese themselves speak of a three-year period of "readjustment," but is it possible that the readjustment could be more permanent?

Three major economic bottlenecks to rapid growth exist in China — agriculture, energy, and foreign exchange. A fourth bottleneck, the rigidity of Chinese bureaucratic management and planning, is a problem that may prove to be more and more crippling as time passes.

There are many aspects of China's agricultural bottleneck, but the core difficulty is that China is trying to feed nearly 1 billion people with only 100 million hectares (247 million acres) of arable land. The United States, with less than a quarter of China's population, has more than half again China's arable acreage. It is not that China makes poor use of the land that it has. Yields from the nation's rice paddies, where water is plentiful, compare favorably with those in other agriculturally advanced nations. Yields in China's northwest are not high by international standards, but water is in such short supply in much of the north that it takes great effort to get anything at all out of the soil.

Other nations, such as Japan and Korea, that have land endowments no better than China's have increasingly turned to imports to meet their food requirements. It will not be long, for example, before half of all Japan's food needs come from abroad. Half of China's grain consumption would be 165 million tons, an amount that China could not possibly afford to import from abroad either now or in the future. Thus, China must meet its domestic food requirements out of its own meager resources.

The single positive element in the Chinese food picture is the decline in the rate of growth of population. The forthcoming census will provide us with more reliable figures, but current estimates indicate that China's population growth rate has fallen from the 2 percent rate of the past two decades to an average of 1.2 percent a year in 1978 and 1979. Offsetting the impact of declining population growth on food demand, however, has been the decision to improve worker and farmer incentives by allowing income and hence per capita food demand to rise. Taking the effects of rising incomes and falling population growth together, it is likely that China over the next two decades will have to maintain a growth rate of agricultural output averaging 3 percent a year. The failure to achieve a 3 percent rate would not lead to a massive expansion of imports – China simply cannot afford to use most of its foreign exchange in this way – but to the rationing of food and to problems with worker incentives, because higher wages would not purchase a higher standard of living, at least with respect to food.

Can China achieve a 3 percent annual agricultural growth rate? The average over the past quarter century has only been 2 percent, but that includes the 1958–1962 period of stagnation and worse. Using 1963 as a base, China has managed a 3 percent annual growth rate. Can it continue to do so in the future? The answer is probably yes, but the cost will be high. One part of the solution would be to solve the north's water problem. Some indication of how expensive a solution may prove to be is given by the fact that Chinese planners are now talking about trying to divert some of the water of the Yangze River to the north. A way must also be found to remove the silt from the Yellow River so that the more limited flow of that river can be used for irrigation. If the water problem can be solved, the task of developing plant varieties with higher and higher yields at China's agricultural research institutes will remain. Despite the damage done to China's research efforts by the Cultural Revolution, there is every reason to think that Chinese plant scientists are up to this task. The Chinese had short-stemmed, high-yielding varieties of rice, comparable to those developed at the International Rice Research Institute in the Philippines, even before that institute was established.

Thus, China will probably manage to meet its food requirements over the next two decades, but large investment funds will have to be diverted to low-return agricultural projects and the whole process will take time. The impact will be to drag China's overall growth rate below what nations like Japan or Singapore, which could avoid dependence on a domestic agricultural sector, could achieve.

The energy bottleneck is one that many developing nations have had to face ever since the Organization of Petroleum Exporting Countries (OPEC) raised the price of petroleum in 1973. For a time, it appeared that China was a major beneficiary, not a victim, of the OPEC price rise, and that may still prove to be the case. Euphoric forecasts that China would soon become one of the world's great oil exporters, however, are unlikely to be realized anytime in the 1980s.

For a decade and a half China did maintain annual growth rates in petroleum production of 15 to 20 percent. Coal production, however, did not fare so well, and most of China's petroleum was used to fill the gap between the country's rising demand for energy and what China's coal mines could supply. The problem was not a lack of reserves – China's coal reserves are huge – but difficulties in getting coal out of the ground with backward techniques and in getting the coal to end users with an overburdened transport system. China's other major energy resource, hydroelectric power, has barely been tapped, with only 2 percent of the nation's potential currently utilized. Petroleum output, therefore, reached the respectable figure of 2 million barrels a day by the late 1970s, but only 10 percent of this total was exported, mainly to Japan.

In 1979 and 1980, China's high rates of growth of petroleum output came to an end as the major onshore fields reached capacity levels. At the same time, China broke with the practices of the past and began to bring in the international oil companies to start exploration for oil offshore. No one, however, expects that offshore exploration will have immediate results great enough to meet all of China's growing energy needs and leave a large surplus for export. Chinese petroleum officials speak of the early 1980s as years of exploration, not of increased production. Conservation and rising coal output must close the short-term difference between supply and demand.

Although China has energy problems greater than were anticipated in the mid-1970s, the shortages should be kept in perspective. Many other developing nations have seen their import bills soar as oil prices rose, forcing these countries to go heavily into debt simply to stay even. For China, the issue is whether there will be a smaller or larger surplus left over with which to earn foreign exchange.

The modest increases in petroleum output are one cause – but not the most important cause – of China's third bottleneck, foreign exchange. Historically, China has earned foreign exchange mainly by exporting agricultural products and, to a lesser degree, minerals and from the remittances of overseas Chinese. As I have indicated, however, China has had trouble maintaining an agricultural growth rate that keeps up with domestic requirements. Thus, agricultural exports have had to be taken out of already short domestic supplies. Under the circumstances, rapid increases in exports of farm output, just like rapid increases in petroleum exports, would soon lead to severe domestic shortages. The problem was not acute in the 1960s and early 1970s because Chinese import requirements were growing slowly, but the development push of the late 1970s and early 1980s has meant a large spurt in imports of machinery, steel, and other key investment goods.

One way out of this foreign exchange shortage would be for China to borrow what it needs abroad. China has already established lines of credit of more than US $20 billion with Japan, France, Britain, and others. Membership in the IMF and the World Bank should give access to further substantial funds, possibly at low interest rates if China qualifies for International Development Association (IDA) loans. But for the most part, borrowing is only a short-term solution to China's foreign exchange problem. Most loans have to be paid back with interest, and although for a time more can be borrowed in order to pay back old loans, eventually China must increase its exports or risk having to cut back on imports and jeopardize its development program.

If agricultural output and petroleum exports will not grow fast enough to meet China's foreign exchange needs, there are still exports of manufactures, particularly manufactures that do not make substantial use of agricultural inputs. In the 1960s, the Chinese began selling cotton textiles in quantity abroad, and in the late 1970s, they partially severed the connection between textile production and the size of China's domestic cotton crop by relying increasingly on imported cotton and synthetic fibers. But textiles face severe trade restrictions throughout the industrialized world, so the potential for export growth is limited. Other manufactures, from electronics to machine tools, also face import restrictions in some cases, but the potential for growth here is greater. China can clearly produce great quantities of bicycles, radios, and much else. The main uncertainty is whether China can manufacture items with the quality and styling required by affluent Western and Japanese markets. Chinese industry at present is geared to producing low-quality goods for a captive low-income market. The conversion to high-quality goods will not be easy and has already led China to experiment with joint ventures and other methods of doing business that only a few years ago were anathema to the leadership.

Finally, in any list of constraints on rapid Chinese growth, one must at least mention the stifling effects of bureaucratic rigidity. The issues are too complex to be dealt with adequately here. They involve questions of whether authority over economic decisions should be in the hands of the provinces or of Beijing, whether the Soviet system of physical planning and allocation should continue to be the norm or whether market forces should play an expanding role, and many others. Western businessmen coming face to face with the Chinese bureaucracy have sometimes concluded that because they found it difficult or impossible to get anything accomplished, the Chinese must also be paralyzed. The Chinese also agree that there are serious planning and management problems, but thousands of projects still get started and finished and output continues to rise. The experience of the Soviet Union with a similar system suggests that the most serious problems lie ahead, when China's economy is larger, more complex, and more affluent.

We might conclude from this list of bottlenecks or constraints that the prospects for rapid Chinese growth are not bright. A closer look, however, suggests that these bottlenecks are the kind that any nation faces in the course of economic development. Japan and South Korea, for example, face far more serious energy shortages than China does, and yet both countries have achieved extraordinarily high sustained growth rates. Elsewhere, major political explosions partially caused by extreme inequalities in income distribution could bring rapid growth to a halt.

Focusing on bottlenecks also tends to obscure the underlying strengths of China's economy. China's rate of capital formation is currently 30 percent or more of gross national product, an extraordinarily high rate even for a wealthy nation. The rate, in fact, may be so high that it has contributed to the lack of worker incentives, but the key point is that most developing countries have the opposite problem – a rate of capital formation too low to carry out the projects that make growth possible. Recent criticisms of China's labor force (often in comparisons with the Hong Kong labor force) obscure the fact that China has already trained tens of millions of skilled workers, foremen, and engineers with the demonstrated ability to run a modern economy. Even when under constant political attack, it was these people who kept industry moving ahead at the rate of 9 percent a year. Now that they are free from political attacks and able for the first time to draw uninhibitedly on the accumulated technological experience of the industrial capitalist world, these managers, engineers, and workers should be able to do even better.

A 7 percent GNP growth rate and an even higher industrial growth rate, therefore, is not a pipe dream; it is a reasonable forecast. As with any forecast, this one is subject to a substantial margin for error, but the margin for error is not all in one direction: China could grow at a rate even higher than 7 percent. Whether it will or not, or whether it will even reach the 7 percent figure, depends on how successful China's leadership is in overcoming the major potential bottlenecks listed here.

Implications for China's Neighbors

What are the implications of another decade or two of rapid growth for China's neighbors? To the leaders of the Soviet Union, with its long border with China, the implications have appeared ominous. It was not always thus; Soviet leaders in the 1950s made the decision to help start China's drive to build a modern steel and machinery industry. For a time, the Soviet Union even helped China develop its nuclear technology. For more than two decades, however, Soviet leaders have looked on China's growing economy and military might with foreboding. With respect to China's nuclear power, there has apparently even been some consideration in years past of a preemptive attack.

It is doubtful that a preemptive attack ever made any sense, even from the narrow perspective of Soviet fear of China. But whatever sense such an attack made in the past, it becomes less and less reasonable as time passes and the Chinese power to retaliate grows. It is paradoxical that what the U.S.S.R. fears most, the rise of China as a superpower, may in fact have the effect of increasing stability along the Sino-Soviet frontier.

The implications of growing Chinese economic strength and

military power for the various nations of Asia are diverse. Japan, which sees expanding trade opportunities and a growing power that can help block Soviet expansion, regards Chinese growth as an unmixed blessing. Thailand and the Philippines share some of the Japanese perspective on growing Chinese power. In particular, Thailand sees China as a major deterrent to continued Vietnamese expansion in Southeast Asia. The Thais may not be completely happy with the prospect of having a superpower on their northern border in the not too distant future, but whatever fear may exist is secondary to the very immediate Vietnamese threat.

At the other end of the spectrum is Vietnam, which can only regard growing Chinese economic and military power as a threat. The current alliance with the Soviet Union helps solve Vietnam's security problem in the short run, but over the long run a policy of flagrantly attacking vested Chinese interests is likely to appear ever riskier. India under Indira Gandhi probably shares some of the Vietnamese perspective. A powerful China is not likely to directly attack India, but India's freedom of maneuver vis-à-vis neighboring Pakistan and Bangladesh might be severely circumscribed.

In between are such nations as Indonesia and South Korea. Indonesia has little to gain from growing Chinese economic power, but neither does it have much to lose from growing Chinese military power. Like India, Indonesia is simply too big to be taken over by a foreign power. Memories of the 1965 coup are still reasonably fresh in the minds of some Indonesian leaders, however, and while those memories remain strong, Indonesia will think of China as more of a potential threat than a potential ally. These attitudes are reinforced, as they are in Malaysia, by fear and dislike of the nation's own Chinese minority.

South Korea's problem with growing Chinese power is related to China's close relations with North Korea. It is doubtful that the South Koreans have much fear of China's acting on its own. Their fear is rather that the Chinese will get dragged into a war by actions initiated by North Korea. Thus, if North and South Korea could moderate their differences, the China problem from South Korea's standpoint would also disappear.

Finally, there is the special case of Taiwan. For the people of Taiwan, growing mainland power is seen as a threat to their continued separate existence. But if economic growth brings affluence and some political liberalization to the mainland, that growth may also facilitate a future peaceful reunion.

Thus, with the exception of Vietnam, no country in Asia lives in great fear of rising Chinese economic and military power. Nations such as India or Indonesia may not look on Chinese developments favorably; neither are they consumed by fear of the potential danger. Why, then, is the attitude of the Soviet Union so different from that of most of China's Asian neighbors? Fear is equally strong on the Chinese side. Only the question is raised here. The answer presumably lies in historical attitudes and much else that is beyond the scope of this chapter.

Implications for the United States

The United States, rather surprisingly, given the past three decades of Sino-American relations, is today in a position vis-à-vis China close to that of Japan. China's economic growth provides opportunities for expanded trade, and rising Chinese power is for the most part a contributor to Asian political stability. There are a few clouds on the horizon. Korea could blow up, dragging China and the United States in on opposite sides, and Taiwan's future is not yet settled. A war between China and the Soviet Union would be in nobody's interest, but the potential is there as long as Vietnam is determined to expand and China is equally determined to resist by means that include force. For the most part, however, Chinese power in Asia is increasingly a guarantor of the right of independent Asian states to set their own courses, and that has long been the goal of U.S. policy in the region. A future Chinese government could use its new power in a more aggressive fashion, but there is little in the historical record to suggest that Chinese leaders in the 1990s would do so.

Even if some future Chinese leadership might turn in a more expansionist direction, that is no reason to limit U.S. ties with the current leadership. Closer ties are the only means the United States has to influence future Chinese leaders to continue on their present course. U.S. policy will not determine the outcome of what is basically a question of the internal political development of China, but a U.S. effort to keep China at arm's length and to treat China as if it might soon again become an adversary could become a self-fulfilling prophecy. Remaining aloof from China because of U.S. fear of the Soviet Union could have the same effect.

For more than two decades – until the steps in the early 1970s to begin the process of normalization of relations – U.S. policy toward China was the hostage of short-term considerations, most of which in retrospect appear trivial. It is time that U.S. policy toward China was made on the premise that the People's Republic is not only the largest country in the world but is destined to be one of the great powers on this planet within a generation.

Bibliography

Dernberger, Robert F., ed. *China's Development Experience in Comparative Perspective*. Cambridge: Harvard University Press, 1980.

Fairbank, John K. *The United States and China*, 4th ed. Cambridge: Harvard University Press, 1979.

Perkins, Dwight H., ed. *China's Modern Economy in Historical Perspective*. Stanford, Calif.: Stanford University Press, 1975.

0520
7180
China

2

China's New Social Fabric:
Views of Inside from Outside

Godwin C. Chu
Francis L. K. Hsu

What is the new social fabric in rural China since the 1949 revolution? Just as in the past, the local communities are a major component. These communities, however, are now embodied in the communes, subdivided into production brigades and production teams. While maintaining some degree of autonomy, local organizational units are woven into a national fabric through two major threads: the administrative channels that are built around the core of the Party structure and the mass media, which provide channels of two-way communication between the center and the local communities.

In this chapter, using mass media materials from China, we shall trace the continuity in the basic structural features that link rural communities with the national system, significant changes that have taken place in rural communities since the downfall of the Gang of Four, and finally some of the problems of the cadre system, which must play a key role in China's modernization.

Continuities in Systemic Organization

The basic unit within which task-oriented cooperation and competition take place in rural China is the production team, generally a natural village or part of one. The production team collectively owns its land and other resources and organizes its members, both men and women, into small groups for various kinds of production activities. Families in the team are assigned private plots, about 5 to 7 percent of the arable land available, which can be used for growing

Copyright © 1980 by the East-West Center.

vegetables, raising poultry, and the like. From among themselves members of the team elect several cadres, including a leader, an accountant, a cashier, a warehouse keeper, and a work point recorder. The cadres serve a term of one year and may be reelected. Usually they are peasants experienced in production and trusted by their fellow villagers.

Several production teams make up a production brigade, and several brigades make up a commune.[1] The commune-brigade-team structure, introduced after 1958, has remained largely intact following initial readjustments. The production team is the basic accounting unit; it produces food and other crops and distributes them among its members after deducting expenses and reserves and selling a portion to the state. The team leader and other cadres generally work along with other peasants in the field in addition to attending to administrative duties. Brigade and team cadres draw no salaries, although they may receive more work points than other peasants, but cadres in the communes hold salaried positions and as a rule do not perform manual work. Under state planning, production quotas are assigned to the communes by higher authorities and are further allocated to the brigades and teams.

Communication Linkages

The communes and the brigades and teams under them are linked with the central government through an intermediary administrative structure consisting of counties, districts, and provinces. Routine administrative directives travel down from the central government through this administrative structure to reach the communes, proceeding from there to the brigades and teams. More intensive communication occurs in the administrative structure when action programs are to be carried out. What vividly distinguishes the present system from its predecessors is the two-way communication along three new channels. Two of the channels are embedded in the administrative structure: first, the dissemination of central documents, which Kenneth Lieberthal has described,[2] and second, the work team, the structure and functions of which have been examined by John Burns.[3] The third channel is the mass media.

Central Committee Documents. Central Committee Documents are a major means by which the leadership in Beijing regularly reaches beyond the confines of the bureaucracy to communicate directly with the mass of the people, including the peasants, to inform them about major decisions and to enlist their support. These documents, codenamed *Zhongfa*, cover a wide range of subjects, from new government policies to political campaigns – generally matters about which the people should be informed but public dissemination of which is considered either inappropriate or premature. Lieberthal has shown how the abortive coup of Lin Biao was explained to the people in this manner without having to expose the whole case through the media. After the resolution on accelerating agricultural development was officially announced on October 6, 1979,[4] it was revealed that a preliminary draft had been adopted ten months earlier and disseminated as a Central Committee Document to the grassroots level for study and discussion.[5] Some of the new measures were tried out on an experimental basis in selected areas. Responses were sought from rural cadres and peasants before a final decision was made. Comments were found to be highly favorable: "This is the best document we have seen in years," or "it is like a timely rainfall during a drought," or "this is what the people want."[6] Thus the central documents not only serve informative functions, as in the Lin Biao case, but can also facilitate input into the decision-making process to garner a broader base of popular support.

The Work Team. The work team as a social institution dates back to the early years of the Chinese Communist revolution. During the Land Reform of 1950–1952, numerous teams of cadres were sent to the villages to organize the peasants in a class struggle against the landlords.[7] Over the years, work teams have played a role in almost every major campaign, whether to investigate local corruption, as in the Four Cleanups movement,[8] or to promote production, as in the Learn from Dazai movement. In both roles work teams perform concrete linkage functions for the government and the local communities, sometimes also fulfilling interest articulation functions, as Burns has illustrated.

Work teams have continued in wide use since 1976, but their functions have come under considerable scrutiny. Doubts have been raised as to whether the dysfunctions may outweigh the benefits, particularly when the work teams are used to promote production. A county cadre in Anhui Province did an investigation in February 1979 by surveying the 308 production brigades in Dangtu County, where he worked.[9] From 1970 to 1977, 178 brigades had been assigned work teams to help the peasants learn from the Dazai experience. The remaining 130 brigades did not have work teams sent to them. During that period, while those brigades that had work teams increased their production by 37.3 percent, those brigades that did not have work teams increased their production by 42.8 percent, 5.5 percent higher than the former.

"The work teams did a lot of work in the villages. Why were the practical effects not satisfactory?" the report asked. Three explanations were given. First, work team members are mostly inexperienced in agriculture. They were cadres at the county level sent to the villages in rotation. When county cadres were insufficient for village assignment, they were joined by schoolteachers, accountants, factory workers, store clerks, and even cooks. They did not understand the nature of farm work and sometimes made hasty personnel changes in the production brigades and production teams that disrupted production.

Second, the work teams in that county were organized into three shifts, each staying in the villages for one year. There was no continuity in the work from one shift to another. Each work team was concerned with production increase only in that particular year, without any long-range planning. Some work teams brought in loans for the purchase of machinery and fertilizer in order to increase production. At the end of the year they walked away, leaving behind unfinished tasks and unpaid loans.

Third, coordination between the work teams and the commune was not clearly defined. Ideally, the two should have worked together through the Party organization to which both belonged. In reality, some work teams functioned under the communes, while others acted as superiors. Even in those cases when the two coordinated their work as equals, lengthy meetings took up much time. The result was much confusion and inefficiency.

The report reaffirmed the positive role of the work team but warned against its misuse. When work teams should be sent, what their membership should be, what purposes they should serve and for how long — these are practical questions that can only be answered by analyzing the actual needs.

The Mass Media. The mass media are another important linkage in China's overall communication system. In addition to providing routine reports on policy announcements, major speeches, official visits, and foreign news, the media play a catalytic role in focusing public attention on the key issues the Party leadership wants to promote, generally in the form of campaigns. The *People's Daily,* for instance, has been giving extensive coverage since mid-1977 to practical problems in the current Four Modernizations campaign. On February 9, 1979, the day Vice Premier Deng Xiaoping returned from his visit to the United States, the *People's Daily* published an editorial urging the Chinese to push wholeheartedly the Four Modernizations.[10] In 1979 and 1980, it ran a special column titled "Contribute Your

Wisdom and Strength to Four Modernizations," in which successful experiences of factories and communes in different regions in improving production and raising income were regularly reported and mistakes by cadres at various levels were brought up for criticism. These features continue, and letters to the editors are published to spotlight problems that have otherwise escaped attention.

One problem with the media is credibility. It has now been admitted that much of the domestic coverage during the 1970s, when the radical group was in power, was false. This was revealed by the *Da Gong Daily*, a Hong Kong newspaper that generally reflects Beijing's official thinking.[11] Quoting an editorial in the *Liberation Army Daily* of November 14, 1977, the report said most Chinese newspapers during the reign of the Gang of Four were filled with empty words. Since then, according to the *Da Gong Daily*, a movement has been afoot to reform China's newspapers and to restore the spirit that Chairman Mao encouraged during the Yenan days.

In July 1979, nearly three years after the purge of the Gang of Four, the *People's Daily* made an unusually candid report in an editorial entitled "Defend Truthfulness, Oppose False Reporting."[12] Since the arrest of the Gang, the editorial said, many newspapers had made an effort to correct false reporting, but in practice, reports that were untrue or only partly true still appeared in the newspapers now and then. Other cases showed selective omission. For instance, said the editorial, a factory had been completed, but due to insufficient power supply and lack of raw materials, production had yet to begin. The news report mentioned the successful completion of the factory without a word about the problems that held up production. Sometimes a report was essentially true but, because of the use of hyperbole, suffered from a lack of credibility.[13]

"These practices of false reporting and exaggeration," said the editorial, "have caused serious damage to the enterprises of our Party. They corrupt the Party's workstyle, and affect the Party's reputation. . . . We have suffered a great deal because of this." Part of the problem, the *People's Daily* said, lay with some of the leadership cadres, who liked to cover up their mistakes and give the reporters only the bright side of a situation. Even when the incorrect report had been exposed by readers, cadres did not want to cooperate with the investigation team from the newspaper and refused to make corrections.[14]

Other changes are also noteworthy. Instead of giving concentrated publicity to a few stereotypes, such as the Dazai Brigade, the *People's Daily* now publishes reports on a wide range of cases of production improvements and income increase from many diverse units and even individual peasants. One gets the impression of a growing concern with factual reporting and pragmatism, especially since 1979.

Local Changes Since 1976

Changes in the Commune

In the countryside, where the roots of the Chinese system lie, important changes have begun to take place since the purge of the Gang of Four. The commune system was established in 1958 on a pattern of localized collective production and distribution. The radical policies pursued during the reign of the Gang, however, have had the effect of smothering the individual work incentive of the peasants without gaining the full benefit of collective productivity. One factor, which we shall discuss later, was the rigid restrictions imposed on family-based productive activities that were likely to boost the peasants' cash income. Another factor was the tendency of administrators at the commune level to draft labor and funds away from the production teams, thus depleting resources for production at the grassroots level. An example of such practices was revealed in a special report published in the *People's Daily* on March 31, 1978.[15] Based on a fact-finding investigation conducted around Tianjin by a correspondent of the *People's Daily*, the following conditions were revealed: (1) Commune enterprises used production team labor without compensation—in one case, 238 laborers in a commune at one time. (2) The same commune employed laborers from the production teams for work in the commune on dike construction. The wages of these laborers were charged to their respective production teams. (3) The commune also used public funds, up to 100,000 yuan in 1977, for non-productive construction. These funds were originally intended for aiding the poorer production teams in the commune. These excessive demands on the production teams were described as "killing the hen for the eggs." The Chinese peasants, in a word, were living below the standard that they could have attained had it not been for the restrictive policies during the late 1960s and 1970s.

A major objective of the current government is, therefore, to develop the potential of the peasants for improving their livelihood. The new policy is that "the peasants must get rich fast."[16] The urgency of restoring rural prosperity was emphasized at a meeting of agricultural experts in September 1979. China's rural communities, in their assessment, were at a historic turning point.[17] Either agricultural modernization would succeed, or rural China would slide back further into poverty.

The new leadership has pursued two policy changes. One is to restore local autonomy by removing some of the centralized controls imposed by the radical group during the previous decade. The production brigades and teams in the communes are no longer required to follow rigidly the production quotas handed down from the central government. Nor are they bound by the previous policy, which concentrated on food production at the expense of other, more profitable cash crops. Now the local units are encouraged to use their resources in the most productive manner as long as the overall production guidelines are followed. Interference from higher levels is discouraged. The other policy change is to allow the peasants more room for material incentives by pursuing family sideline activities within the general framework of local collective production.

A symbolically significant step to accentuate the new policy is the revamping of Chairman Mao's "In Agriculture, Learn from Dazai" movement. Xiyang County, home of the Dazai Brigade, made a thorough examination of the Dazai model in August 1979 and came up with several recommendations. The private plots, which in Xiyang used to be allotted to small collective groups under the Dazai model, have now been given back to individual families. Family sideline production, previously considered a form of small capitalism, is now encouraged. Trees around the houses have been returned to the families. The Dazai model of group evaluation of work points has been replaced with more specific criteria. In food distribution, those who work more will get more. This replaces the Dazai model known as "eating from a big bowl," by which each family declared its needs and these were then assessed at group meetings. The result was a more or less even distribution regardless of work input.[18]

We shall illustrate the new policy on material incentive with two examples, both given national publicity in the *People's Daily*. In the Zhenhu Brigade outside Shanghai, a commune member, Fan Zaigeng, cleared a net profit of 5,900 yuan in 1978 from a variety of sideline productions. His family of nine worked together, both before and after commune hours, and became rich. There were criticisms by other members of his brigade because his sideline profit far exceeded his family income of 1,872 yuan from commune work. The *Wen Hui Daily* of Shanghai, however, endorsed Fan's enterprising spirit: "There is absolutely nothing wrong if a peasant can get rich by working hard." Fan, the paper pointed out, did not exploit anybody, did not steal or rob, and did not let his collective assignment suffer.[19]

In the Xishan Brigade of Xinchang County in Zhejiang, commune member Yuan Zhenghua raised rabbits as a sideline, feeding them with grass cut from a nearby hill by his children. In one year he made nearly 1,000 yuan. In comparison, the total wages his family earned from the commune that year were some 370 yuan. The *People's Daily* told this story in a positive vein.[20]

By the spring of 1980, the new policy began to pay dividends in terms of increased income among peasants. Although no overall statistics are available, we shall cite Kuihu Commune in Sichuan Province as an example. Production Team No. 4 in that commune was a relatively well-off village. Before the new policy, the average annual per capita income of that production team was around 70 yuan, not including income from private plots, which ranged from 5 to 20 yuan per capita depending on individual families. After the new policy came into effect, the average income rose to 354 yuan per capita for 1979. In addition, the families were earning sideline income ranging from 200 to 400 yuan per person a year.[21]

Under the new policy, the Chinese government recognizes that it is inevitable that some peasants will get rich faster than others. The point is that not everybody can get rich at the same time, said the *People's Daily*, and this fact should not prevent some peasants from making the best of their resources within the collective framework.[22]

Degree of Local Autonomy

The Chinese peasants seem to be catching on fast to the new emphasis on material incentives, but restoring autonomy to the production brigade and team has proved more difficult. One problem was how far local autonomy should go. During the 1979 spring planting, soon after central documents spread the word of local autonomy, some production teams in northern China began adopting practices that threatened to weaken the foundation of the commune system. This was revealed in a letter to the *People's Daily* by Zhang Hao, a cadre, following his visit to Luoyang in Henan Province.[23] Zhang learned that many production teams in that area either had already adopted or were about to adopt a practice known as *baochan daozu*. That is, members of the production teams organized themselves into "mutual aid teams," each consisting of six or seven families totaling about forty to forty-five people. Land, farm tools, and cattle that belonged to the production team were divided up and assigned to the mutual aid teams. In some communes, even the reserve grains were distributed to the mutual aid teams. Each mutual aid team was to work on its portion of land, assume responsibility for its production quota, and keep what was left.

Zhang was told that this was only the first step. The next step would be to assign all production means, including land, and production quotas to the individual families. There was apparently pressure from the county to push this new measure, but Zhang said some cadres at both the production brigade and the production team levels had told him about their reservations. There was concern about the effect on agricultural mechanization, which requires large-scale operation. What was not mentioned in the letter was the implication that if land and other means of production were distributed to the families, then the system would return to the days after the Land Reform in the early 1950s, when individual farmers were given their own land to work on.

This practice of small team operation was apparently not unique to Henan. A similar case was reported in Jilin Province.[24] In Nanweizi Commune, one production team had 101 laborers in eighty-five families working on 1,900 *mou* (313 acres) of land. In early 1979, they divided themselves into three small operation teams, each having its own land, farm tools, and cattle. The plan was for each operation team to dispose of its autumn crops after contributing its share of reserve grains. When the Party secretary of the commune learned about this, he went to the production team and organized the members to study the two central documents on agriculture. which had apparently been misinterpreted. The central documents had encouraged the formation of small operation teams as a more flexible and efficient way of using manpower, but not as an accounting unit for the distribution of income. The error was corrected in time, the report said.

The *People's Daily* in a special comment praised the Nanweizi commune Party secretary for this action. Production teams were encouraged to work out their own utilization of resources, but, said the official daily, "the communes should not hastily change the basic accounting unit under circumstances when the [required] conditions are not present."[25]

The initial solution was to combine a division of labor suitable to small operation subteams with a distribution of reward that remained in the context of the entire production team. This solution is known as *wuding wutong* (Five Fixed Factors, Five Coordinations): A fixed number of laborers work on a fixed area of land, for fixed assignments, to produce a fixed amount of crops of fixed quality, under fixed criteria of reward and punishment. The production team coordinates (1) leadership, (2) calculation (of cost) and distribution (of crops), (3) production plans, (4) manpower utilization, and (5) use of cattle and tools.

Each production team is to work out a definite pattern of division of labor and distribution of reward with a minimum of interference from outside. This is to be achieved by organizing the production team members into task subteams; each subteam is given its portion of land and other means of production and required to produce a quota of grains at the end of the year according to an overall plan. The small subteam is not allowed to keep its surplus production but will be given bonus wages as an incentive. The production team is still the basic accounting unit, but the small production unit is expected to simplify management and the bonus incentive, to increase productivity. This new policy is a significant step away from the concept of large collective production and distribution.

The experience of a production team in Henan shows why these operational guidelines are necessary.[26] During the period from 1974 to 1976, when the Gang of Four was in power, production teams had followed a policy under which more work did not result in more work points. As a result, "the peasants went to the field when it was already high noon and scored ten points just by idling around." When the new policy was first introduced, however, the peasants were so eager that they fought for stronger cattle and better tools and scrambled for those assignments that required little labor but produced more work points. The guidelines on Five Fixed Factors, Five Coordinations were intended to minimize these tendencies.

Throughout 1979 and 1980, the Party leadership continued to experiment with different forms of agricultural production and income distribution, according to a report released by the official Xinhua News Agency in May 1981.[27] In the spring and summer of 1980, the Party's leadership cadres in Beijing went to villages across the country, from Yunnan in the southwest to Liaoning in the northeast, for on-the-spot investigations. The Party's Central Committee and the prime minister's office later commissioned more than 100 rural workers and economists to conduct a two-month survey in villages in ten provinces. Both Prime Minister Zhao Ziyang and Hu Yaobang, secretary-general of the Central Committee, made field trips in early 1981. Afterward a special session was held at the Party's Central Secretariat on March 2, 1981, to review the findings.

A key topic was the feasibility of a practice known as *baochan daohu*, which Liu Shaoqi once successfully employed in 1961 to stimulate a recovery of agricultural production following the initial fiasco of the People's Commune movement. The idea was to assign production quotas not to production teams but to individual families. The family was allowed to retain the extra crops beyond the fulfillment of the quota. This practice was tried out by Liu in various locations for a couple of years. It was severely criticized by the radical group during the Cultural Revolution.

In mid-September 1980, the first Party secretaries of all provinces, major municipalities, and autonomous regions met in Beijing to discuss the feasibility of this practice as a means of promoting agricultural production. A central document issued on September 27, 1980, reaffirmed *baochan daohu* as a practice not inconsistent with socialism as long as it is implemented under the supervision of the production team. Vice-Chairman Deng Xiaoping was quoted by Xinhua as endorsing this practice in principle for economically backward areas where land is vast and population sparse. Some of the survey results presented to Deng showed doubling of peasant income after this practice was tried out for one year.

Prime Minister Zhao, in summarizing his own field trip observations, suggested three alternative ways of organizing agricultural production that appear to be the bases of an emerging new policy. The three alternatives represent different degrees of collectivism, depending on the strength of the local rural economy.

In areas where the foundation of collective rural economy is solid, and agricultural production and the standard of living have been improving, agricultural production should continue to be assigned to small task subteams (*zuoyezu*) on a collective basis. Under the overall planning and supervision of the production team, these subteams are to be organized on a voluntary basis to perform specific production tasks, such as rice growing or vegetable production. A task subteam will work and share production responsibility collectively according to a contract signed with the production team. The production team will coordinate the income distribution. If a subteam exceeds the production quota specified in the contract, it will receive extra income for distribution among its members. If a subteam fails to fulfill the quota, a penalty will be assessed. Of the three alternatives, this one is a form of higher collectivism.

In rural areas where the economy is at an intermediate level, collective work management will be given more flexibility. People will still work in small subteams, but production responsibilities will be assigned to individual laborers, not to the subteam. Income will be distributed on the basis of individual task fulfillment within the subteam context, with extra income for extra task achievement by the individual. This form allows more individual incentives within a collective framework of resource utilization.

In relatively backward areas, *baochan daohu* can be practiced to allow individual families to be the units of production assignment and income distribution. A family will receive from the production team its share of land to till (not to own) and will work on its own according to a family production quota rather than on a subteam. The family income will depend entirely on its own production. After fulfilling its assigned quota in terms of contribution to the state and setting aside reserves for the production team, the family keeps everything for itself. It also has to absorb losses, if any. Another difference from the two previous alternatives is that cadres in the production team will have to earn their income through labor like everyone else, instead of getting work points by performing supervisory duties, as few are required under *baochan daohu*. According to comments from some peasants, this system will get rid of blind commandism from above and do away with the practice by which cadres take away the fruit of the peasants' labor. In some areas, after *baochan daohu* had been practiced for one year, rural family income went up considerably. Several families then got together and pooled their resources to buy major farm implements, cattle, and small tractors.

These alternatives, including *baochan daohu*, refer to agricultural work on land collectively owned by the production teams. In addition, rural families have been allowed to work on their private plots and engage in sideline productions. The Chinese farmers apparently wanted various forms of production management and diverse sources of production revenues, said the Xinhua report. The Party's Central Committee was considering appropriate readjustments in agricultural organization in order to achieve diversification of rural income.

In another policy statement on the eve of the Sixth Plenary Session of the Party Central Committee in June 1981, Vice Premier Wan Li made the following remarks:[28]

- The people's commune system had reached a point of change and reform. Although the Chinese peasants had not yet rejected the commune system, the extent of collectivism in the system was currently under review. Two basic socialist principles had to be upheld. First, there could be no buying or selling of land. Second, there must be no exploitation. Within these contexts, the original concept of combining government administration and production in a single commune organization was being modified. A major problem in the past had been excessive administrative interference with production. One possible solution would be to place agricultural production under the management of a separate joint enterprise, the nature of which was to be specified.

- The degree of collectivism would be relaxed. The size of the private plots (*ziliudi*), estimated in the spring of 1981 to be about 5 to 7 percent of all arable land, would be expanded to 15 percent. It had been noted that in some areas the productivity of the private plots had increased by as much as four to six times in the previous few years. Even on land that was collectively cultivated, the peasants would be given the autonomous right to change their crops in order to suit the market needs.

• Another major change being considered would allow an unspecified percentage of peasants (*ziliuren*) to depart from collective labor and work exclusively on private plots.

These changes, when implemented, will in effect move the agricultural production system close to the days of the mutual aid movement in the early 1950s after the agrarian Land Reform.

Reluctance to Innovate

Some local cadres are afraid to pursue any innovative practices for fear that they might be criticized for deviating from the correct ideological line. The *People's Daily* cited the following case as an illustration.[29] During the heavy snow in the spring of 1979, a production brigade in Hebei Province assigned the care of its sheep and lambs to individual families to save the animals from starving and freezing to death. Those who took care of the sheep earned work points. In the fall of 1979, two production teams proposed to continue this practice on a regular basis. The Party secretary of the brigade stopped them, however, and asked the commune leadership for approval. The commune said no.

A reader who wrote to the *People's Daily* listed all the advantages of individual family care of sheep. "But because it involved individual families [*hu*]," said the reader, "nobody dared to give his approval." In a brief comment, the *People's Daily* asked: "Why is it so?" "We should no longer be bound by the restrictions of the past," said the commentary, "but should encourage the mass of people to learn from practical experience. Our policy is to promote production. We should stimulate the enthusiasm of every family to seek ways of production increase. Otherwise, does it mean that we are pursuing socialism if we herd the sheep together and let them freeze and starve, and that we would be pursuing capitalism if we assign the sheep to individual families and let them grow well?"[30]

The issue of ideological line, or "direction" (*fangxiang*), has apparently been a major stumbling block to agricultural production. "In the villages," said the *People's Daily*, "we often hear people say: 'This practice is fine, and can stimulate the enthusiasm of commune members. We are just afraid that the direction might not be correct.' Or: 'This is what the people would like to see, and we are sure grain production will increase. But we are afraid of making an error about the direction.'"[31]

Under the general premise of collective ownership, said the official daily, the correct direction should be to increase production. But because of the overwhelming leftist influence of the past, the term "direction" had taken on many "mysterious interpretations." The *People's Daily* gave a few examples:

- If a family raised two chickens, it was socialism; if a family raised more than two, it became capitalism.
- If a family raised pigs and sheep it was socialism; if a family raised a cow, it became capitalism.
- If there was barren land outside the village and you simply let weeds grow there, it was socialism; if you assigned the land to individual commune members for cultivation and food production, it became capitalism.

The result was that both cadres and commune members lived in constant suspense, fearing that they might have done something that violated the correct direction. To liberate productivity, said the *People's Daily*, the Chinese must emerge from their ideological bondage and smash the arbitrarily concocted standards of false socialism.

Abuse of Authority

Another problem that has impaired local autonomy is the reluctance of cadres at the county and commune levels to relinquish the authority they have become accustomed to exercising. Since 1978, the central government has repeatedly emphasized that production teams must be allowed to work out their own production plans. But such instructions are sometimes ignored.

In Ningde, Fujian Province, when winter planting came in early 1979, the district cadres simply did what they had always done before: They took out the old quotas, which were often unrealistic, and sent them to the production brigades and production teams. This time, the peasants began to complain. They called it "the same old style of commandism" and "blind exercise of leadership." In this case, the district cadres went to the fields to listen to the peasants and revised their production plans.[32]

An incident in Hebei was not resolved so smoothly. Peasants in a production brigade in Liucun Commune had planted watermelons and cucumbers,which were not specified in the production plans. Just before the crops were ripe, the cadres in the commune found out about them and ordered the peasants to pull up the melons and cucumbers and destroy them. Furthermore, the commune cadres punished the brigade with an additional assessment of 5,000 catties

(5,510 pounds) of grain for that year.[33] Within a week of the first report on this case, many readers wrote to the *People's Daily* to condemn what they considered to be "rotten behavior of blind leadership" and the serious bureaucratism that some cadres still manifested. Even though two central documents from Beijing had encouraged sideline family production and allowed the production teams flexible wage guidelines under the new policy of local autonomy, one reader said, these directives were ignored by commune cadres in some places.[34]

The destruction of melons in Liucun Commune was apparently not an isolated case. A similar incident, it was revealed, occurred in Shandong in 1975 when the radical group was still in power. A production team had planted 15 *mou* (2.5 acres) of melons. Upon learning this, the commune cadres sent a team to destroy all the melons and dismissed the production leader. Even though the commune cadres now realized their error, they still considered it beneath their status to admit their wrongdoings in front of the peasants.[35]

The *People's Daily* condemned the latest melon case in a special commentary. "What is serious is not the loss of some 10,000 yuans worth of melons at Liucun Commune but rather the obnoxious attitudes of a small number of commune cadres toward the people and their benefits," said the official paper. What the Liucun Commune cadres destroyed was more than tens of acres of melons: "They destroyed the normal relations between our Party and the people."[36] The Liucun commune incident, the *People's Daily* said, revealed that some cadres like to act like "officials sitting on the heads of the people." The ills of the old feudalistic mentality still prevailed. The melon incident sounded a bell of alarm, demonstrating the necessity and urgency of a healthy democratic system.[37] The paper cited an official government report by Chairman Hua Guofeng:

> Our country has a long history of feudalism. Our economic civilization is relatively backward. And we have not properly propagated and implemented democracy in the past. Our system is not adequate. Under those circumstances, autocracy, bureaucratism, special privileges, and head of family style have readily spread. . . . [Therefore] the various leadership cadres in the communes should in future be elected by the mass of people.[38]

The Shijiazhuang District Office, which has supervisory responsibility over Liucun Commune, took the following measures:

1. It directed the county secretary to send a senior-level cadre to Liucun Commune to help its cadres correct their attitudes. The

production brigade that had suffered a loss because of the
destruction of melons was encouraged to engage in a variety of
types of production so that it could increase its income and
make up for the loss.

2. It distributed an account of the Liucun melon case to all units in
the district for discussion and criticism.

3. It organized a campaign to study the two Central Committee
Documents on the new agricultural policy that had been
violated by the Liucun Commune cadres.[39]

The serious discrepancy between the new policy guidelines and
their implementation at the local level is underscored by another case
that came to light at the time of the melon incident. On August 3,
1979, the *People's Daily* published a news release from the official
news agency Xinhua, which shows how following the new
agricultural guidelines could be misinterpreted as a rightist
deviation.[40] At Yangjiaping Brigade in Hubei, some peasants had
responded to the new guidelines by planting cucumbers and bamboo
shoots around the houses. They were scared when told that such practices amounted to capitalism. Even though most of them hastened to
destroy the plants overnight, they were subject to group criticism.

What is noteworthy about this case as an illustration of communication failure is that the misinterpretation resulted from four days of
meetings of county and commune cadres to study the two central
documents on agricultural production. What was originally intended
to be encouragement for production increase through local autonomy
came out as criticism of capitalism. The rationale of the cadres was
this: Because the guidelines did not mention planting cucumbers and
vegetables around houses as an acceptable form of production, then
anyone doing that must be practicing capitalism.

In an editor's note, Xinhua said the Yangjiaping case must not be
dismissed as a minor issue. It showed how deeply rooted was some of
the leftist thinking imposed by the Gang of Four. Serious, continual
criticism would be necessary, the editor noted, before things in the
villages could be managed well.[41]

Reform of the National Cadre System

The key to the current Chinese system is the cadres. They are the
links between the Party leadership and the people. They transmit
directives from the central government to the grassroots. They have
the responsibility of organizing the mass of people for action programs

and of transmitting feedback to the Party leadership. The flow of communication, horizontal as well as vertical, downward as well as upward, lies primarily in their hands.

Revelations made since the purge of the Gang of Four have pinpointed many flaws in the cadre system, most of which appear to be inherited from traditional Chinese bureaucracy. Cadres at various levels formed themselves into cliques and factions to protect each other, an old custom known as *guanguan xianghu.*[42] Efficiency and performance were often of little consequence. In many organizations, an official report said, it made no difference whether one did a lot or little, a good job or a poor job—or indeed whether one did anything at all. Cadres were employed not because of their abilities, but because of personal relations.[43]

Part of the problem lies in the tenure system for cadres. For instance, in the two and a half weeks after its first report on the melon incident, the *People's Daily* received more than 240 letters from twenty-one provinces and municipalities.[44] Many letters said the reason why cadres of Liucun Commune could totally ignore the interests of the peasants was that their jobs were like an "iron rice bowl" (*tiefanwan*) that is, indestructible. Whether the peasants in a production team were rich or poor was of no concern to them; their positions were always secure. If the commune cadres were popularly elected, and if the people had supervisory power and could dismiss them, said the letters, the situation would be different.

Reeducation of Cadres

To remedy these deficiencies, the Party has taken several measures. One is a campaign, launched in the summer of 1979, to reeducate the cadres and instill in them a new sense of the revolutionary fervor destroyed by the Gang of Four. An editorial in the *People's Daily* on August 15, 1979, stated that those old cadres who had suffered at the hands of the Gang should not use their past grievances as an excuse for special treatment. Nor should the younger cadres consider themselves a privileged class.[45] The editorial cited a historical anecdote to teach the cadres a lesson. After the founding emperor of the Tang Dynasty died, there was an internal struggle for the succession, out of which his second son emerged as Emperor Taizong. His minister, Wei Zheng, sensing a trend of arrogance and lassitude, spoke bluntly with the emperor. He advised Taizong to curb his desires, suppress his arrogance, prevent laxity, invite criticism, resist flattery, and avoid favoritism. Emperor Taizong took his advice. "These are provocative thoughts for the leadership cadres of our ruling Party," said the editorial. "Shall we not expect these of our leadership?"

As part of this campaign, the Party encouraged the people to expose the erroneous behavior of their cadres and bring it up for public criticism. Soon after the editorial, the *People's Daily* publicized the case of Sanho County. Sanho, in Hebei Province, suffered severe damage during the earthquake of 1976. The situation was aggravated by a flood in 1977 that affected the crops. Some 3,400 commune families were homeless and lived in makeshift tents. The county's Party committee, however, commandeered free labor from the production teams to build a new auditorium. Following this example, seven communes and more than ten county agencies began a spree of building new offices. Someone wrote a letter to the prime minister's office that received the attention of Chairman Hua Guofeng. Hua condemned the Sanho cadres and sent the case to the provincial committee for action. Meanwhile, the Party's Central Committee disseminated a report on the errors of Sanho to all units in the nation as a negative example to be avoided.

On August 23, 1979, nearly a year and a half after the first exposure of the Sanho case, the official daily reported that the county cadres had accepted the criticisms of the mass of people and corrected their mistakes. All construction projects not related to production had been stopped. Some 600 laborers drafted from the production teams had been returned to agricultural work. Funds and materials commandeered from the production teams had been returned. Some of the new houses built by the communes had been given to those families who were in need of help.[46] In an editorial accompanying the story, the *People's Daily* remarked that the wicked trend demonstrated in Sanho was a symptom of feudalism. Chairman Hua's instruction had been to "criticize this wicked trend." "However," said the official daily, "there are still those cadres who consider themselves always right. In their region or unit they are the king, the lord. Even when they are clearly wrong, they would not listen to the slightest criticism from the people. A tiger's backside must not be touched. They storm into a temper if anyone attempts to criticize them. . . . This is completely wrong."[47]

A New Model

The Party leadership is using a variety of media, including short stories, drama, and television plays, to create a new image of cadres. The official paper endorses the new image and emphasizes that this is the way the cadres should behave. We shall cite one short story, "Director Qiao Returns to His Job," as an example.[48]

Director Qiao Guangpu exemplified the ideal cadre for the Four Modernizations now being pursued by the Party. A Party member of long standing, Qiao suffered from persecution during the reign of Lin Biao and the Gang of Four, at one time even being "sent to live in the cowshed," a Chinese idiom for exile and labor reform. His wife died under ambiguous circumstances. But Qiao did not indulge in self-pity. Now that he was back in his old post as director of a heavy-duty generator factory, he would not let anything stand in the way of production increase. In the factory he faced all kinds of bizarre obstacles, but he was not to be stopped. He was determined to run his factory in a pragmatic and scientific manner despite the opposition and complaints of some of his subordinates.

In contrast, the first Party secretary at the factory, Ji Sheng, was portrayed in the story as an opportunist who typified a trend known as *fengpai*, that is, following whatever direction the wind is currently blowing. Ji, also an old cadre, liked to brag about how he was persecuted by the Gang of Four. He had no real ability but was smooth in personal relations, good at sensing his superiors' preferences. He constantly surveyed his environment, even relying on rumors and "alley news" (*xiaodao xiaoxi*) to determine how he could best adapt and survive.

Although clearly condemning the first Party secretary, the story showed more sympathy than blame for another senior cadre, Shi Gan. Formerly Party secretary at the factory, Shi had worked with Director Qiao closely twenty years before, when both were young. But the many purges during the day of Lin Biao and the Gang of Four left him exhausted and disillusioned. He learned his lesson, so to speak, and now approached any problem with extreme caution. Sometimes he even pretended not to see the problem.

Commenting on this story, the *People's Daily* praised Director Qiao for his courage and pragmatism, and disapproved of the first Party secretary. The tired and dejected Shi was seen as typical of many cadres who could be reeducated and revived.

Evaluation of Cadres

In addition to the education campaign, the Party is looking for concrete ways to evaluate the cadres. In his 1979 administrative report on the work of the government, Chairman Hua said: "We must establish an adequate system governing the examination, evaluation, supervision, reward and punishment, and dismissal of cadres so that our cadres will not degenerate from public servants into overlords who ride over the heads of the people."[49] Such a system of evaluation is necessary not only because of the many ills of bureaucratism we have already noted, but also because "the incompatibility between the current cadre system and the Four Modernizations is becoming more and more striking," as the *People's Daily* put it.[50] The evaluation has been tried out in urban areas and is expected to be applied in rural regions later.

The experience at the machine shop in Tsitsihar, Heilongjiang Province, gives some indication of the merits of the new evaluation system.[51] The evaluation, which was tried out in the winter of 1978 and the summer of 1979 on some 270 cadres at the section-chief level, used three main categories: qualifications for the job, level of performance, and ideology and workstyle. Of these, level of performance had the greatest weight. For technical staff, this evaluation was to examine the output of the section and the cadre's contribution to the work output. For managerial staff, it was to rate their performance in organizing production activities. For cadres in the Party organizations, it was to evaluate their effectiveness in implementing the policies of the Party and in coordinating relations with the mass of people, as well as their ideological work.

The evaluation was based on personal interviews, input from the workers and other units related to the cadre, output statistics, and other results of the investigation of the cadre's achievements and shortcomings. Each cadre was to be evaluated twice a year, and an overall rating was to be given after two years. Four ratings were to be used: superior, satisfactory, in need of improvement, and disqualified. After a trial for one year, 14 of the 270 cadres were found to be disqualified and were demoted. Another 12, also considered disqualified, were retained on probation. Four cadres were found superior and were promoted to leadership positions.

The machine shop said its one-year trial evaluation had three major results. First, it enabled the leadership cadres to know their staff more thoroughly and thus to make more efficient use of manpower. Second, it provided an incentive for the cadres to strive for efficiency because superior performance was rewarded and inadequate work was punished. Third, it prompted the cadres to seek professional improvement lest they be left behind their colleagues.

Improving Communication

The Party has continued to stress better communication between cadres of higher and lower levels and between the Party and the people. An editorial in the *People's Daily* suggested that all leadership cadres make an effort to talk to their subordinates.[52] Some leadership cadres, said the official paper, are either indifferent or impatient.

Lower-level cadres may have something concrete to suggest or questions to ask. But if a leadership cadre is reluctant to see them, then good work cannot be done. Talking to lower-level cadres can have five benefits, the editorial continued. One gains firsthand information, which can counterbalance one's own bias. One can learn something from one's subordinate. The leader can get to know his subordinates. Talking to one's subordinates can avoid misunderstanding and promote unity, and above all, it can help overcome bureaucratism.

The *People's Daily* gave some concrete suggestions on how to talk to subordinates: Don't always talk to the same people; find some new faces to talk to. Treat subordinates as equals; don't act like a boss. Use rational analysis, not authority, to convince subordinates. On important matters, don't deviate from the basic principles. Finally, be patient. If one conversation brings no result, try again.

The Party has emphasized again the linkage function of letters and visits from the people. Such direct contacts are considered vital to the campaign against bureaucratism.[53] But there are leadership cadres, said the *People's Daily*, who treat the letters and visits as trivial matters. Letters from the people are piled up for a long time and not given any attention. When people visit their offices, the cadres refer the complaints elsewhere or even suppress them. As a result, some people have had to take a long journey to the provincial capital, or even to Beijing, to file a petition. The behavior of these cadres is detrimental to the unity and stability of the country, said the official paper.

According to the *People's Daily*, Hua Guofeng and other leaders in the central government have personally read many letters from the people. Hua has given the following instruction in his government report: "The leaders of all government offices and enterprises must pay careful attention to the cries of the people, and be concerned with their ills and woes. They must personally handle the letters and visits." Even anonymous letters are not necessarily bad, said the *People's Daily*. As long as the motivation is constructive and the contents are factually true, anonymous letters should be welcome. "After all, how a citizen wants to express his opinions and requests is his democratic right. Nobody should interfere."[54]

General Observations

Local Solidarity

Given the scope and complexity of the subject matter and the limited nature of our data, we do not make any claim to definitive conclusions. The observations that follow are thus tentative. Even though many important details are still unavailable, however, the general picture can be sketched with only a marginal degree of ambiguity.

The building block of China's contemporary society is the local village, as it has always been. One fundamental difference between the present and the past is the removal of exploitation, primarily by the landlords in league with the bureaucrats in the cities, many of whom were landlords themselves. Today in the production teams, which are mostly natural villages, the peasants and the team cadres, who are themselves peasants elected by their peers, share a sense of solidarity. This solidarity has been built partly on the traditional foundation of kinship-oriented in-group relations that have always existed in Chinese villages. Economically, these relations were reflected in the traditional custom of mutual help known as *hutong youwu*, that is, sharing now what you have with others who will someday share with you what they have when you are in need. This custom has now been institutionalized in collective ownership and distribution in the production teams.

Ideologically, the Chinese peasants have always looked upon their villages as the extent of their worlds. Although their political horizons have now been enlarged, their immediate concerns are still with their own villages, their own production teams. The transition from the traditional, landlord-dominated village to the collective production team has been an arduous process. Through trial and error, the Chinese peasants have worked out a system under the Party that combines the collective with the private, in production as well as distribution.

We shall cite two cases to show that this village solidarity, the cornerstone of social integration, is based on traditional roots of local identity and shared local interest. One is the case of the destruction of melons. The reports in the *People's Daily* did not mention how the decision to plant the melons was reached in the production team, but it was apparent that the team cadres were on the side of the peasants. They did nothing to stop the peasants. The interference eventually came from cadres in the commune, who were outside the village. The other case involved what could be a major departure from the commune system, when one production team in Nanweizi Commune started to divide up its land, farm tools, and cattle into small operation teams that would then be allowed to dispose of their own crops. This action, which could be the first step toward dissolving the commune system, could not have been taken without the support of the production team cadres. It was the commune secretary, again someone from outside the village, who stopped it.

This *communal solidarity*, rooted in traditional local identity and shared economic interests, provides the basis for collective, task-oriented cooperation in the production teams. It sometimes enables local groups to fend off administrative encroachment from outside. It is this same local solidarity that has enabled the vast rural Chinese population to withstand such spasmodic convulsions as the Cultural Revolution. It kept the Chinese villages beyond the destructive arms of the Red Guards. It provided many local cadres with an umbrella of protection against the wanton deeds of the young rebels. It enabled the villages to survive the restrictive policies of the radical faction. In short, it helped keep China's social fabric intact.

Although this local solidarity grows out of traditional roots, its new form has been strengthened by two important developments, one substantive and the other communicative. The substantive development was the land reform programs of the early 1950s that eliminated exploitation by the landlords. This action put the resources for production into the hands of the Chinese peasants.[55] The communicative development occurred during the many campaigns of the last three decades. Even though some of the campaigns caused temporary disruptions to village life and production, they have had the latent effect of linking the villages to a national system of communication. They allow the central government to penetrate the local units and achieve an "identification between the ruler and the ruled," as Alan Liu has phrased it.[56] This process has proved to be essential to political socialization. Many Chinese peasants have come a long way from their past ignorance and submissiveness to become articulate and outspoken members of the village community. They participate in the management of their production teams in their roles as commune members. There is even a tendency for some of them to speak out on affairs beyond their villages, as indicated by letters published in the official paper. They are no longer a "tray of loose sand," as Dr. Sun Yat-sen once ruefully called them.

The melon incident illustrates anew a basic principle of social integration in China that has been demonstrated time and again in history: that is, local autonomy is essential to the stability and welfare of Chinese society. The Chinese village fares best when external demands and interference are held to a minimum. This is why rural China was thrown into such chaotic dislocation when the commune system was introduced in 1958 in its initial form.[57] The degree of collectivism, under which villages were to be controlled by the huge communes, would have irretrievably destroyed village autonomy. The disaster was relatively short-lived because enough members of the Party leadership quickly realized the errors and made the necessary readjustments. Much local autonomy was soon restored under Liu Shaoqi's policy, known as *sanzi yibao*.[58] When the radical groups regained power after the Cultural Revolution, which saw the ouster of Liu, they again tried to take away some local autonomy. The result of the rigid centralized control was a slowdown of agricultural productivity. The new leadership in Beijing has been working to undo some of the damage caused during the ten years when the Gang of Four was in power. The new policy is to help the peasants get rich by allowing the production team considerable leeway in planning its production and managing its distribution.

The policy of Five Fixed Factors, Five Coordinations, under which the production team can divide itself up into small operation teams (for production but *not* for distribution) already gives the villages more autonomy than they have had since the agricultural cooperative movements of the 1950s. The manner in which the *People's Daily* commented on the Nanweizi Commune case, however, seems to imply that more changes may be forthcoming. As we may recall, the *People's Daily* had said that the communes "should not hastily change the basic accounting unit under circumstances when the [required] conditions are not present."[59] This statement leaves the door ajar for such a change, if and when the as yet unspecified conditions are present.[60] The policy statement issued in May 1981 was a step toward such a change.

New Social Fabric

China's new social fabric is made of strong local fibers closely woven into a central pattern directed from Beijing. Institutionalized in the production teams, the local fibers are as earthbound as their predecessors.[61] But unlike the villages of the past, the production teams of today are securing an increasingly autonomous base for the management of their own affairs. The agrarian land reform of the early 1950s eliminated the pervasive economic and political influence of the landed gentry, removing a perennial source of rural exploitation.[62] In place of the gentry, a new crop of village leaders has risen from the ranks of the peasants. They now manage the use of local resources, work out task-oriented cooperation, and distribute rewards. Their ascendance to positions of local decision making is an important feature of China's new social fabric. It has opened up avenues of social mobility and altered the relatively fixed social relations that existed in Chinese villages for generations.

Life in traditional rural China was marked by an atmosphere of static harmony and nonaction; the production teams today are characterized by incessant action programs of all kinds, each requiring the exposure and subsequent resolution of conflicts. The subjects of conflict have included the landlords in the early 1950s, various cliques in the 1960s and early 1970s, and now bureaucratism. Indeed it is the resolution of such conflicts that gives the production teams a measure of vitality. It is through the implementation of action programs by the new village leaders and their team members that a dynamic integration is maintained in the local communities.

The Chinese villlage no longer struggles for its survival in virtual isolation. Not only is there frequent lateral communication with other production teams and brigades in the same commune, but an elaborate communication network, through administrative channels, Central Committee Documents, work teams, and the mass media, links the production teams into an integrated national entity. The flow of communication in the network is primarily downward. But the local units at times are able to send feedback upward, mostly complaints against excessive interference by cadres immediately above them but also statements of support for government policies, such as the one on agricultural development.

Although the Party has stressed the necessity of allowing the people to seek redress by bringing their complaints directly to leadership cadres at higher levels, through either letters or personal visits, this policy has not been fully implemented. A more accessible channel, one that is becoming far more effective since the purge of the Gang of Four, is the mass media, particularly the newspapers. Individuals with personal grievances or divergent opinions on local problems can and do write to the *People's Daily*; they often receive immediate attention. Even major policy issues, such as the stigma of individuals' undesirable class identification, have been recently contested through letters to the editor; policy changes sometimes ensue.[63]

Both the *People's Daily* and the official news agency Xinhua report on some of the basic issues facing the production teams, such as the heavy financial burdens imposed by the communes, or premature trends, such as production teams' planning to divide themselves into even smaller operation teams. Both the letters and the investigative reporting by the media are significant channels by which the interests and concerns of the common people can be communicated, horizontally as well as upward to top-level policy makers. We have seen how letters to the editor have touched off public outcry, followed by action by the authorities to correct mistakes. The letters column is thus more than a safety valve that prevents accumulated tension from reaching an intolerable level. It provides a mechanism for conflict resolution and serves as an instigator of reform in the organizational structure that may eventually lead to modification of the structure.

The institution of the mass media is among the major structural features that distinguish the current Chinese social system from its traditional predecessors.[64] Because of the nearly total absence of such communication channels in the past, not only was the old Chinese social system never closely integrated,[65] but the imperial court was usually unaware of mounting unrest until it was too late. Traditional China did have its ombudsmen, the *yu shi*, and sometimes especially courageous officials like the legendary Judge Bao, who had an imperial mandate to correct injustice on the spot. But they were too few and their efforts too sporadic to be effective. In this perspective, the mass media as an institution are of critical importance to societal integration in China not only because they are powerful instruments for mobilizing and coordinating national efforts, but also because they can be a major mechanism of checks and balances to prevent the abuse of power.

China under communism has retained and strengthened integrative features of local communities. But it has also built up an extensive communication network to incorporate these local communities into a national entity. The basic structural foundation for this new integration has been laid. Although each major rectification campaign in the past twisted or dented the national network, the local communities have remained largely unscathed, thus preventing the system from falling apart despite such turmoils as the Cultural Revolution. The recent shift of policy from ideological indoctrination to pragmatic development has posed new challenges to the Chinese system. Will the national communication network be used to its full capacity to mobilize the Chinese people and thus meet the requirements of the Four Modernizations? The basic issue, as the melon incident seems to suggest, is this: How do Party cadres reorient their thinking and style of operation to carry out the new tasks? The prospects of an invigorated process of societal integration to gain a higher plateau of national achievement depend on the way this issue is resolved.

Notes

1. For a description of the Chinese commune system, see William L. Parish, "Communist Agricultural Organization: China—Team, Brigade, or Commune?" *Problems of Communism* 25 (March-April 1976):51–65. For a model commune in the early 1970s, see Chu Li and Tien Chieh-yun, *Inside a People's Commune* (Beijing: Foreign Languages Press, 1974). Brigades and communes

are primarily administrative units. In general, cadres at the brigade level are nominated by the production teams and appointed by the commune leadership; cadres in a commune are appointed by the county. At each level, from the commune down to the production team, Party organization parallels the cadre structure. Not all cadres are Party members, although the more responsible positions, particularly from the brigade level up, are likely to be held by members of the Party.

2. Kenneth Lieberthal, "Communications from the Party Center: The Transmission Process for Central Committee Documents," paper presented at the Conference on Communication and Societal Integration in China, East-West Center, Honolulu, Hawaii, January 1979.

3. John P. Burns, "Peasant Interest Articulation and Work Teams in Rural China: 1962–1974," paper presented at the Conference on Communication and Societal Integration in China, East-West Center, Honolulu, Hawaii, January 1979.

4. "Resolution of the Chinese Communist Party Central Committee on Certain Issues Related to Accelerating Agricultural Development," *Renmin Ribao* (hereafter *People's Daily*), October 6, 1979.

5. "A Strong Impetus for Accelerating Agricultural Development," editorial, *People's Daily*, October 7, 1979.

6. For example, see "Team Leader Yin Did Right," *People's Daily*, February 5, 1979. This document apparently reached down to the peasants; in a number of disputes with leftist-inclined local cadres, said the report, the peasants cited it as a basis for their demands for greater autonomy. The same report shows how speedily central documents are disseminated. Soon after the dissemination of this central document on agricultural development, several peasants in Hebei took some fish from a commune fishpond without authorization. When the production team leader asked them for compensation, they refused on the grounds that the central document said that wanton deductions and fines should not be imposed on the peasants. In this case, the peasants misread the central committee document to justify their action.

7. See Godwin C. Chu, *Radical Change through Communication in Mao's China* (Honolulu: University Press of Hawaii, 1977), pp. 35–60.

8. See Richard Baum and Frederick C. Teiwes, *Ssu-Ching: The Socialist Education Movement of 1962–1966* (Berkeley: Center for Chinese Studies, University of California, 1968).

9. The following is based on Lu Tao-sheng, "Do Not Misuse Work Teams," *People's Daily*, February 5, 1979.

10. "Wholeheartedly Push the Four Modernizations," editorial, *People's Daily*, February 9, 1979.

11. Cai Ji, "Newspapers in China Are Undergoing a Major Reform," *Da Gong Bao* (hereafter *Da Gong Daily*) (Hong Kong), December 7, 1977.

12. "Defend Truthfulness, Oppose False Reporting," editorial, *People's Daily*, July 24, 1979. Some reports were fabrications, said the editorial. For instance, on February 22, 1979, the *People's Daily* published a correspondent's report on an irrigation project in Anhui, where, it said, "more than 40,000 workers and

engineers have been battling a severe snowstorm since last December to construct a permanent irrigation station." As it turned out, the editorial stated, far from employing 40,000 workers, the project had not even been started.

In another case, the *People's Daily* published on December 13, 1978, a feature story on the death of a revolutionary martyr, Wei Bagun, about which it had this to say: "Before his execution, Wei told his wife to have faith in the ultimate victory of the Party and resolutely carry on the struggle. He took off a button from his clothes and asked his wife to give it to the Party as his last membership fee. Then, his chin firmly up, he walked to the execution ground." "In fact," the July 24, 1979, editorial said, "comrade Wei was shot during his illness by a renegade. Such untruthful sensationalism has no place in our news reports."

13. "Defend Truthfulness, Oppose False Reporting," editorial, *People's Daily*, July 24, 1979.

14. Ibid.

15. "Let's See How Many Unreasonable Burdens Are Carried by Production Teams," *People's Daily*, March 31, 1978.

16. "How Can We Make the Peasants Rich as Quickly as Possible?" *People's Daily*, August 9, 1979.

17. "Our Nation's Agriculture Has Reached a Historic Turning Point," *People's Daily*, September 11, 1979.

18. "Xiyang County Discusses the Pragmatic Basis of Truth for the 'Learn from Dazai' Movement," *People's Daily*, October 3, 1979.

19. "Fan Zaigeng, a Commune Member, Earns Nearly 6,000 Yuan from Family Sideline Production," *People's Daily*, August 9, 1979; also, "A Faultless Income of 6,000 Yuan," *Wen Hui Bao* [Wen Hui Daily] (Shanghai), August 6, 1979, reprinted in *People's Daily*, August 9, 1979.

20. "Yuan Zhenghua Makes Nearly 1,000 Yuan from Raising Rabbits," *People's Daily*, August 25, 1979.

21. "How Do We View the Increased Income Among Some Peasants?" *People's Daily*, April 20, 1980.

22. Ibid.

23. "Stabilize the System of Three-Tiered Ownership, with Production Team as the Foundation," letter by Zhang Hao, Bureau of Records, Kansu, *People's Daily*, March 15, 1979.

24. "Nanweizi Commune Party Secretary Corrects the Error of Using Operation Team as the Accounting Unit," *People's Daily*, March 15, 1979.

25. Editor's note, *People's Daily*, March 15, 1979.

26. "Fixed Work Management Results in Production Increase," *People's Daily*, March 31, 1979.

27. The following is based on a special report released by Xinhua News Agency on May 20, 1981. The report was originally carried by *Liaowang* [Forecast], a magazine published in Beijing, in its May 1981 issue, under the title of "Constantly Thinking of the 800,000,000 Peasants." It was in a special column reporting on activities of the Party's Central Committee. This particular report covered the 88th regular meeting of the Party's Central Commit-

tee Secretariat. It was carried in *Da Gong Daily* (Hong Kong), May 20, 1981. See also "A Major Change in Chinese Villages," *Da Gong Daily*, June 16, 1981.

28. "Wan Li Discusses Reform in Agriculture and People's Communes," *Da Gong Daily*, June 6, 1981.

29. "How Come Nobody Would Give His Nod to Such a Good Practice?" *People's Daily*, April 20, 1980.

30. Ibid.

31. Nan Lan, "On 'Direction,'" *People's Daily*, April 28, 1980.

32. "Abandon Commandism, and Modify Winter Planting Program," *People's Daily*, February 10, 1979.

33. "What Does the Destruction of Melons Case Mean?" *People's Daily*, July 27, 1979. Also, *Hebei Daily* Comments on Destruction of Melons in Liucun Commune," *People's Daily*, July 31, 1979.

34. "Cadres and Commune Members in Hebei Express Anger over Destruction of Melons," *People's Daily*, August 1, 1979; also "Strong Reactions from Readers in Henan to Destruction of Melons Case," *People's Daily*, August 1, 1979.

35. "Mingji Commune Cadres Discuss Destruction of Melons Case," *People's Daily*, August 3, 1979.

36. "On the Incident of Destruction of Melons," *People's Daily*, August 3, 1979.

37. Ibid.

38. Ibid.

39. "Shijiazhuang District Office Issues Statement on Destruction of Melons Case," *People's Daily*, July 31, 1979.

40. "A Down-to-Earth Policy Must Not Be Mistaken for Capitalism," *People's Daily*, August 3, 1979.

41. Ibid.

42. "Evaluation of Cadres Must Be Done," editorial, *People's Daily*, August 8, 1979.

43. "The Practice of Using Relatives Must Be Avoided," *People's Daily*, August 15, 1979. The official daily revealed some of these practices. For instance, when some leadership cadres were transferred, they brought not only their immediate families, but also secretaries, chauffeurs, maids, and family members. Others found ways to transfer close to them not only their grown-up children, but daughters-in-law, sons-in-law, and even their sons' fiancées.

44. "Readers Express Anger, and Ask Provocative Questions on Destruction of Melons Case," *People's Daily*, August 20, 1979.

45. "Strict Demands for Our Leadership Cadres," editorial, *People's Daily*, August 15, 1979.

46. "Directly Face Mistakes, Courageously Make Corrections—Sanho County Secretary Accepts Criticism," *People's Daily*, August 23, 1979.

47. "The Revelations of Sanho," editorial, *People's Daily*, August 23, 1979.

48. "The Four Modernizations Need Leaders Like Him—Comment on the Short Story 'Director Qiao Returns to His Post,'" *People's Daily*, September 3, 1979.

49. Quoted in *People's Daily*, "On the Incident of Destruction of Melons," August 3, 1979.

50. "Evaluation of Cadres Must Be Done," editorial, *People's Daily*, August 8, 1979.

51. "Cadre Evaluation System Tried Out Among Section Chiefs," *People's Daily*, August 8, 1979.

52. The following is based on "Encourage Conversation with Cadres," editorial, *People's Daily*, July 11, 1979.

53. The following is based on "Leadership Cadres Must Personally Handle Letters and Visits from the People," editorial, *People's Daily*, July 11, 1979.

54. "Are Anonymous Letters Necessarily Not Above Board?" editor's comment, *People's Daily*, July 11, 1979.

55. For analysis of the Land Reform movement, see Chu, *Radical Change*, pp. 35–60.

56. By *penetration*, Liu referred to the process by which the central government reaches regions that hitherto were autonomous. By *identification*, he referred to the process by which the media gradually diffuse a set of common norms, values, and symbols so that identification can be established vertically between the rulers and the ruled and horizontally among citizens and groups. See Alan P. L. Liu, *Communications and National Integration in Communist China* (Berkeley: University of California Press, 1971), pp. 2–3.

57. The initial difficulties in the commune movement have been described in Chu, *Radical Change*, pp. 187–214.

58. Liu Shaoqi's *sanzi yibao* means three *zi* and one *bao*. These are *ziliudi* (private plots), *ziyou shichang* (rural free markets), *zifu kuiying* (assume loss or profit), and *baochan daohu* (production quotas set on families). In other words, this policy allowed commune members to retain and cultivate the private plots and to sell the products at rural open markets. Agricultural production quotas were set for the individual families, not for the collective. The production teams in the communes had to pledge to deliver to the state their shares of taxes and grains. Beyond that, they were free to dispose of their profits or assume responsibility for any loss. Liu's policy contributed to the recovery from the three disastrous years for China's agriculture following the Commune movement of 1958. One major difference between Liu's policy and current practice is that agricultural production quotas are largely set for the task subteams, not for individual families. Liu, who was expelled from the Party in the Cultural Revolution, was posthumously rehabilitated by the Party Central Committee in March 1980. An important treatise written by Liu on the duty of the Party and its members, dated July 1, 1940, was republished in the *People's Daily* in March 1980. See Liu Shaoqi, "How to Be a Good Party Member, How to Build a Good Party," *People's Daily*, March 12, 1980. Liu's standing in the Party has now been fully restored.

59. See editor's note on "Nanweizi Commune Party Secretary Corrects the Error of Using Operation Team as the Accounting Unit," *People's Daily*, March 15, 1979.

60. The basic accounting unit is important because it determines the nature

of the economic system. The smallest basic accounting unit is the individual. (The individual is used as the basic accounting unit in the United States when husband and wife file income tax returns separately.) In rural China today, as far as the private plot is concerned, the basic accounting unit is the nuclear family, as the family members usually work together and presumably share the income from the private plot. We have had accounts in the official paper suggesting how high family productivity from the private plots can be. It seems that moving the basic accounting unit from the production team level to the small operation teams, each consisting of several families, could increase productivity because small units could mean greater material incentives. The eagerness with which such deviations from the official policy were being pursued by some production teams, for instance those in Luoyang, as reported in the *People's Daily*, suggests the benefit that might be derived from this change. The question is whether such a move may end up in a rush back to the family as the exclusive accounting unit for both private plots and agricultural production in general. It would seem that if such a rush could be prevented, the current Party leadership might not be averse to a modification of its commune structure to make the small operation team instead of the production team the basic accounting unit. The former would be a cluster of families; the latter is a village.

61. For analysis of village life in traditional China, see Fei Hsiao-tung, *Peasant Life in China* (London: G. Routledge & Sons, 1939); Fei Hsiao-tung and Chang Chih-I, *Earthbound China* (Chicago: University of Chicago Press, 1945); and Martin C. Yang, *A Chinese Village, Taitou, Shantung Province* (New York: Columbia University Press, 1945). Life in a rural town has been analyzed by Francis L. K. Hsu in *Under the Ancestors' Shadow* (Stanford, Calif.: Stanford University Press, 1971).

62. See C. K. Yang, *A Chinese Village in Early Communist Transition* (Cambridge, Mass.: MIT Press, 1959).

63. See Godwin C. Chu and Leonard L. Chu, "Letters to the Editor They Write in China," *East-West Perspectives* 1:1 (Summer 1979):2–7.

64. Deutsch has made the general observations that the mass media as well as other types of communication are essential to the development of a national community. See Karl W. Deutsch, *Nationalism and Social Communication: An Enquiry into the Foundation of Nationality*, 2nd ed. (Cambridge, Mass.: MIT Press, 1966), pp. 86–106. Irving Allen argued that mass communication is identical and basic to the meaning of mass society. See Irving L. Allen, "Social Integration as an Organizing Principle," in *Mass Media Policies in Changing Cultures*, edited by George Gerbner (New York: John Wiley & Sons, 1977), pp. 235–248.

65. Francis Hsu, for instance, suggested that a near void existed between the central government and the local communities in traditional China. See Francis L. K. Hsu, *Americans and Chinese: Reflections on Two Cultures and Their People*, 2nd ed. (New York: Doubleday, 1970), pp. 375–379.

4200
China; Japan; U.S.S.R.

3
The Great Triangle:
China, the U.S.S.R., and Japan

Allen S. Whiting

Ethnocentric Americans may object to the concept of a "great triangle" that excludes the United States. However, a half century of East Asian international relations reveals a triangle of tension that has locked Russia, China, and Japan into recurring warfare in which the United States, except during World War II, has played a peripheral role. This chronology of conflict deserves recapitulation to remind us of the memory scars that underlie present-day relations among these three powers.

The nineteenth century ended with war between China and Japan. The twentieth century began with war between Japan and Russia. Following the Bolshevik revolution, Japan occupied Siberia and Sakhalin and left Russian soil only in 1925. In 1929, Russian and Chinese troops fought along the Chinese Eastern Railroad. Two years later, Japan seized Manchuria, a prelude to the eight-year Japanese invasion of China. In 1938–1939, Soviet and Japanese armies fought an undeclared war. Finally, in the closing days of World War II, Stalin's forces attacked Japan.

Thus, each of the three nations has fought the other two, singly or in tandem. Each has perceived the other two acting in concert against it, whether by dividing spheres of interest, as with Russia and Japan in China, or in a tacit alliance, like that of the Soviet Union and China against Japan. This heritage of hatred and mistrust continues as each of the three governments is today engaged in a territorial dispute with one or both of the other two.

True, the past is not necessarily precedent. It need not predict the shape of things to come. But the past can structure perceptions of the present and expectations of the future in the minds of policy makers, regardless of nationality or ideology. Memory, reinforced by experience, provides a powerful filter of reality for both ruling elites and

47

ordinary masses. Indeed, these subjective perceptions may prevail over objective facts in determining policy at the highest levels of government. In particular, they can affect the selection of evidence concerning the opponent's true intentions, exaggerating the threat and the degree of danger.

The pessimist—often a self-defined realist—argues that tension is so locked into this great triangle as to be irreducible at best and explosive at worst. This argument has much to support it. For twenty years the Sino-Soviet dispute has sparked armed clashes over the disputed border, with war alarms in both countries. A buildup of Soviet forces on illegally occupied islands north of Japan amid the steady expansion of Moscow's air and naval power in the Western Pacific prevents negotiation of a peace treaty between the two countries and prompts Tokyo to strengthen its defenses. The dramatic reversal of Sino-Japanese relations from conflict and confrontation to friendship and cooperation is marred by China's assertion of ownership over the Senkaku Islands held by Japan. In 1978 more than a hundred armed Chinese fishing boats pressed this claim, to the embarrassment and consternation of the Fukuda government.

Nor does the larger context necessarily conflict with a pessimistic prognosis. China's invasion of Vietnam and Chinese support for the Pol Pot guerrilla forces in Cambodia are countered by Soviet military aid to Hanoi, which is reinforced by Soviet air and naval deployments to the South China Sea. The Soviets and the Chinese exchange propaganda charges of aggression and expansionism, lumped under the code word "hegemony." Meanwhile, Moscow voices suspicion of Sino-Japanese collusion in an anti-Soviet front. Beijing publicizes Soviet military moves around Japan and incites Japanese demand for return of the northern islands. Each side warns Japan to beware of the other.

Those who project a more optimistic future—often pejoratively labeled idealists—argue that economics may ultimately prevail over politics. They suggest that interdependence can gradually defuse the explosive territorial disputes and conflicts of interest. They base this analysis on the fact that capital and technology are increasingly being traded for valuable resources, especially energy, among Japan and its two communist neighbors. The three countries also have a mutual interest in managing ocean resources in Northeast Asia to ensure the optimal exploitation of fish and offshore oil. Optimists, then, have an ultimate vision of a Pacific community based on geographical proximity and practical utility, regardless of political or ideological differences.

Unfortunately, there is no definitive way to determine whether the optimists or the pessimists are right. Forecasting is still a hazardous art, not a systematic science. However, we can at least weigh the prospects for alternate futures on the basis of present trends and logical inference. Against the conventional "worst case" argument of alarm, we have both the right and the obligation to posit a "best case" of hope. Provided that our construct of this future is feasible as well as desirable, we should be able to design policies that advance the likelihood of realizing the best case in addition to policies that protect us against the worst case.

Obviously, I cannot do justice to both approaches in this brief space. Instead I will examine the less familiar of the two cases, namely, the prospects for economic interdependence within the triangular relationship of the Soviet Union, China, and Japan. In particular, I will focus on the future of Siberian development and its implications for Sino-Soviet and Soviet-Japanese relationships.

Sino-Soviet Relations:
Bilateral Tensions and the Border Conflict

Let us take the Sino-Soviet side first. So burdened is this relationship with negative features that it may seem utopian in the extreme to consider possible positive aspects of Siberian development. A twenty-year polemic that embraces virtually all aspects of foreign policy on both sides is paralleled by massive concentrations of military force in confrontation over the 4,650-mile border, which is in dispute. Throughout the Third World, Moscow and Beijing struggle for influence in a competition that brooks no compromise. Their antagonism fuels the continuing Indochina conflict, which threatens to consume Cambodia and may spill over into neighboring land and water.

Yet it is possible to narrow our focus to the bilateral relationship as the most relevant to our explicit triangular concern. Here the picture is somewhat brighter than it was while Mao Zedong was alive. The ideological dispute that lay at the heart of Mao's attack against Khrushchev in the late 1950s and his successors thereafter has, like the famous Cheshire cat, slowly faded away since the chairman's death in 1976. The accusation of heresy embodied in the term "Soviet revisionism" no longer appears in Beijing's propaganda. In fact, last fall one of China's most respected elder figures, Yeh Jienying, admitted that one reason the Cultural Revolution went wrong was that revisionism had been wrongly defined.

Symbolic surrender to Moscow's legitimacy, at least in domestic policy, came this spring when Chinese workmen quietly removed the signs naming the location of the Soviet embassy "Antirevisionism Street." In its place a nonpolitical nomenclature appeared. Superficial as this may sound to non-Marxist ears, it is a significant concession for China to make. For one thing, it means that Beijing is no longer obligated to call upon the Soviet people to overthrow the leadership in Moscow, as was the practice for more than a decade.

A second point of contention between the two capitals has been China's claim that much of the border has not been correctly demarcated and that, as a result, Chinese territory is being illegitimately occupied by Soviet forces. Delimiting and demarcating this lengthy frontier is no easy task, except at its eastern end where the Amur and Ussuri rivers provide a natural line of division. But even here questions arise as to the role of the main channel compared with the river banks, with further complications posed by the numerous islands dotting the waterway. Elsewhere, local herdspeople wander where their livestock take them without regard to the rival claims of distant capitals.

Under such circumstances, hostile incidents are inevitable. Yet judging from the public statements by both sides, no genuinely serious clashes have occurred since 1969. Moreover, conversations with specialists in China and the Soviet Union reveal little anxiety or tension on the matter. This state of affairs is reflected in the failure to publicize minor incidents that nonetheless prompt official protests in private, a point of diplomatic discretion in marked contrast to the tenor of the propagandistic exchanges.

As for the actual areas alleged by Beijing to be in dispute, only two have strategic importance. One is a large uninhabited island at the confluence of the Amur and Ussuri rivers, adjacent to Khabarovsk. The importance of this key transportation and industrial nexus precludes any concession to Chinese claims by Moscow. In 1977, however, Beijing relented a little, negotiating arrangements for river traffic that implied an eventual willingness to abandon this claim. The second area, known as the "Pamir knot," joins the Soviet, Afghan, and Chinese frontiers. Wholly under Soviet administration, this high mountain valley provides access to important passes in various directions. Moscow is unlikely to compromise on this issue either.

Should both sides have the will, however, they can find a way to resolve the remaining border problems. Meanwhile, annual Sino-Soviet negotiations on river traffic keep ships moving without incident. Residents of border cities like Khabarovsk and Vladivostok report no tension or fear of war. Nor has the relatively stable, if high, balance of forces in confrontation changed markedly in recent years. After the initial doubling of divisions on the Soviet side in the late 1960s, a slower but steady expansion has leveled off at approximately 700,000 troops. The upgrading of weaponry now includes the Backfire bomber and the SS-20 missile, significantly strengthening the nuclear capability. But this is still far below Beijing's claim that 1 million Soviet troops threaten China, much less a force sufficient to launch an offensive against the far larger People's Liberation Army. In fact, half the Soviet divisions remain at roughly one-quarter strength.

Siberian Development and Sino-Soviet Relations

The foregoing permits us to examine the implications of Siberian development for Sino-Soviet relations in a somewhat different perspective from that offered by a simple projection of past tensions into a single-line future. Recognizing that these tensions may continue, however, we should assess the negative prospects of Siberian development.

At first glance, the most serious challenge to China's security would appear to be the Baikal-Amur Railroad, or BAM. Virtually a second Trans-Siberian line, its 2,000-mile length parallels the Trans-Sibe but is considerably farther removed from the Chinese border. Upon its completion in 1985–1987, this line will provide a major logistical asset by relieving the overburdened Trans-Sibe of commercial freight and adding another route for military movement.

On closer examination, however, we see that the Baikal-Amur line is of little strategic significance. Highly vulnerable to natural hazards, it cannot be relied upon over any great distance during any lengthy period for regularly scheduled use. It passes through one of the most seismically turbulent areas in the Soviet Union. Moreover, in precisely this portion a system of tunnels, one 9 miles long and another 4, burrows deeply through the permafrost. Permafrost itself magnifies the shock effect of earthquakes. Where the track runs above the ground, it must be separated from the permafrost by a 6- to 8-foot bed of timber or gravel; otherwise the transmission of heat will disturb the underlying support base. This condition prevails over more than half the length of BAM. In addition, landslides and mudslides abound, icing provides a recurrent hazard, and annual flooding requires literally thousands of bridges and culverts. Some 140 of these bridges exceed 300 feet in length, with permafrost requiring differentiated pilings and foundations to allow for the heaving and settling of the subsoil. These conditions combine to make BAM's reliability at particular points and times highly uncertain. In wartime, BAM's vulnerability to airborne attack poses even greater obstacles to military planning.

This set of conditions explains why BAM has proceeded so slowly in the absence of the high-priority crash effort normal for Soviet projects held to have top strategic importance. Announced with nationwide fanfare in 1974, the original target date for completion, 1983, has slipped badly. Although BAM is now 40 percent finished, the most difficult portions remain ahead. Some observers even question whether the post-Brezhnev regime will continue the heavy investment in what promises to be a highly uneconomic venture with uncertain payoff in the distant future. Assuming no major setbacks or changes, however, BAM's earliest date of completion is now estimated to be 1985, with 1987 a more likely time for full operational capability.

No other projects presently envisioned in Moscow should be perceived in Beijing as increasing the potential Soviet threat. Even the term "Siberian development" is something of a misnomer. There are no plans nor is there the capacity to develop this region in the conventional sense of the term, transforming it from a vast frozen wilderness into a modern industrial base of Soviet power in the Far East. The demands on capital, technology, and management to develop the infrastructure necessary to support the increase in population required by such an effort far exceed Moscow's ability and will.

Instead, East and Far East Siberia will be exploited for their natural resources, primarily to earn hard currency through export and secondarily to meet indigenous Soviet demand. This type of development poses no threat to China. On the contrary, it could prove beneficial if the two economies come into a more harmonious and interdependent relationship. Setting politics aside, the natural complementarity of Far East Siberia and northeast China was formerly manifest in their traditional trading relationship. The Soviet side is seriously deficient in foodstuffs; the Chinese side has a surplus. Siberia's virtually limitless timber reserve contrasts with China's desperate timber shortage. A copper field below Yakutia is among the largest in the U.S.S.R.; China's reserves have yet to be adequately established. Even China's staggering surplus labor problem could relieve Siberia's chronic labor shortage.

This relationship won recognition during the heyday of the Sino-Soviet accord. Khrushchev proposed that Chinese workers should provide contract labor in Siberian forests. Mao agreed, and some 200,000 Chinese served in this capacity during the mid-1950s. A joint Sino-Soviet scientific commission devoted eighteen months to surveying the prospects for combined management of the Amur River and its tributaries. Their findings, under the title "Amur — River of Friendship," showed how flood control, navigation, irrigation, and hydro-electric power could result from a massive joint effort.

Viewed in these terms, Siberian development need not weigh negatively in Sino-Soviet relations; indeed, it has positive potential. This circumstance may explain why Beijing's propaganda has remained remarkably muted on the subject for several years, particularly since Mao's death. Japanese firms engaged in building the Baikal-Amur Railroad and other projects deny experiencing any private pressure from Beijing to desist from helping the Soviet program. In fact, the engineering firm most involved with BAM has landed a major contract in China. Equally significant is the fact that the Japanese organization engaged in assisting the Soviet Union to explore for offshore oil near Sakhalin won the first foreign concession for similar activity in Bohai Bay.

Siberian Development and Japan

This takes us to the other leg of the triangle, namely Soviet-Japanese relations. Over the past decade, Moscow has shown increasing interest in bringing Japan (and the United States) into joint development of this remote region's natural wealth. After an initial Japanese refusal to participate in construction of an expensive pipeline to transport oil from West Siberia to Pacific ports in conjunction with construction of the Baikal-Amur Railroad, several major projects have joined the two countries in a common effort. One such project is the opening of a major coalfield in South Yakutia, where $500 million in credit from Tokyo is to be repaid with 5 million metric tons of coking coal annually for fifteen years. To facilitate this export as well as that of large timber and wood chip production for the Japanese market, Tokyo has helped develop the port of Wrangel, the largest Soviet outlet to the Pacific. Another joint effort aims at exploration and exploitation of offshore oil around Sakhalin.

Tokyo's commitment to Siberian development is manifest in the nearly $1.5 billion of credits advanced by the Japanese Export-Import Bank, with another $1.5 billion underwritten by Japanese private banks. Anyone familiar with the history of Soviet-Japanese relations will find this a striking anomaly. Nowhere is this anomaly more evident than in the Sakhalin project. Not only have the two countries competed for control of Sakhalin over much of the past century, the Soviet Far East is seriously deficient in oil, a strategic commodity, requiring shipment of some 10 million tons per year thousands of miles from fields in West Siberia.

Moscow's most far-reaching proposal, in magnitude and implication, is joint Soviet-Japanese-American development of natural gas fields in Yakutia. The initial estimate of $4 billion in foreign investment with a matching Soviet amount has long since been inflated by rising costs and a more sober prognosis of the expense involved in a 2,000-mile pipeline through Siberian mountains and forests, a liquefaction plant at its terminus, liquefied natural gas tankers, and reprocessing facilities at the delivery end. Nevertheless, Japanese interest, both marketing and financial, has remained high. U.S. participation, however, already limited by congressional restrictions on export-import credits to the Soviet Union, has been totally eliminated, at least for the present, by President Carter's reaction to the invasion of Afghanistan.

The caricature of "Japan, Inc." grossly distorts the degree of independence of industry and government in Japan. But clearly nothing so expensive and so sensitive in its implications as Siberian development would be undertaken by Japanese business without close consultation with official circles. Extensive interviews on both sides reveal a highly sophisticated and strong consensus on the political utility of pursuing economic advantage to the point of modest interdependence between Japan and the Soviet Union.

As one official high in the Fukuda cabinet put it, "Security is a major preoccupation of Japan, but it has two aspects, negative and positive. Negative security is military defense against attack. Positive security is economic cooperation to reduce perceptions of threat and hostility. You cannot have one without the other." Another commented, after conclusion of the Sino-Japanese treaty in 1978, "Now it is more important than ever that we continue cooperation in Siberian development. Moscow must not perceive us as colluding with Peking against the Soviet Union."

This policy is particularly striking because it is not a result of Soviet blandishments. On the contrary, heavyhanded Soviet propaganda and diplomacy have continually aroused hostile public opinion in Japan and provided ammunition for the Self-Defense Agency's annual budget appeal. I have already mentioned Moscow's attack on the Sino-Japanese treaty. Since the announcement of the treaty, Soviet forces have been increased on the disputed islands north of Hokkaido; this includes the introduction of tanks and the construction of an airfield. Japanese protests over the military buildup are brusquely rejected with the assertion that this is "purely a domestic Soviet matter," the ownership of the islands allegedly being beyond dispute. Meanwhile, Soviet ships and planes continue to violate Japanese territorial waters and airspace.

In this context, it is small wonder that Tokyo adamantly refuses to negotiate a peace treaty with Moscow similar to that with Beijing. However, Tokyo remains determined to keep economic cooperation moving ahead as a token of political as well as economic interest in better relations. One official explained it in terms of a shift from "equidistance" to "balanced diplomacy." Instead of trying to keep evenly apart from both sides in the Sino-Soviet dispute, "we want to show we are willing to help both sides in their economic development to prove that we are not hostile to either nor can we be pressured by either." Thus, when China finally decided to seek government credits, the Japanese Export-Import Bank opened the window for $2 billion, as it had already done for the U.S.S.R. This official emphasized that "balance" does not mean "equality," noting that "in view of our cultural closeness to China and the complementarity of our two economies, there is no realistic way that we could have exactly the same relationship with our two communist neighbors. But insofar as we respond positively to each in the same way, consonant of course with our own economic interests, we maintain balance in our relationships."

When challenged as to the risks of interdependence with Moscow, Japanese respond with almost universal reassurance. First and foremost, they fail to find any plausible reason for the Soviets to try to apply political pressure through manipulation of the energy flow from Siberia. Second, they point out that a much greater degree of interdependence has already been accepted by NATO countries that are much closer to actual military confrontation with Moscow. Last but not least, they note that at a maximum, including the still unrealized Yakutia gas proposal, the Japanese will not rely on Soviet energy resources for more than 15 percent of their total needs. Moreover, alternative supplies are readily available elsewhere.

Japanese policy clearly differentiates Soviet military and civilian interests. It responds firmly and negatively to undesirable behavior from the former while negotiating patiently but positively on proposals from the latter. Officials admit that there is no certainty this practice will have any results over time, least of all that it will win major concessions, such as the return of the contested islands. But, they see little risk, considerable economic benefit, and at least a possibility that Soviet-Japanese relations will ultimately improve. Finally, they see no such possibility from adopting the U.S. assumptions about linkage and leverage, to be applied through negative economic policies like credit restrictions and technology embargoes.

The Political Framework of Economic Interaction

I began by briefly reviewing the pessimistic prognosis for political confrontation in East Asia against the heritage of hatred and mistrust. But this is not the only trend in the region. Despite the abundance of political problems that directly and indirectly affect the triangle of relations, none is at a high point of confrontation and most exist in quiet limbo as the result of tacit or explicit understandings arrived at in recent years. The most notable example is the Korean peninsula, where a country is divided into two armed camps. Yet in nearly three decades no serious hostilities have occurred, and talks of at least symbolic significance are now under way between the two sides. Tension has wholly disappeared in the Taiwan Strait, in spite of the U.S. renunciation of its defense commitment to the Chinese Nationalists. The Senkaku Islands issue has been indefinitely shelved by Tokyo and Beijing, and the northern islands are not an active matter between Tokyo and Moscow.

The Sino-American detente, the Sino-Japanese peace treaty, a tacit but mutual understanding among the major patrons of the respective Korean antagonists, and the priority given by post-Mao China to internal economic development have combined to place the politics of East Asia in a framework that is less tense than at any time since the end of World War II. Such an atmosphere permits greater attention to the economic interactions, present and potential, relevant to equally critical questions of natural resource management, particularly in and beneath the ocean, capital and technology flows, and possible interdependence. This explains why Japan, alone among the major nations of the region without nuclear weapons and with only a token conventional force, has gradually emerged to play a major role. Its needs and its assets complement those of its neighbors in a mutually reinforcing way, provided that economics are permitted to prevail over politics.

It may be that behind Chinese rhetoric are groups who see this reality. Sino-Soviet trade continues its modest but steady increase, including suggestive items like medium-range jet transport and helicopter aircraft. In 1979, Beijing agreed to meetings at the deputy-foreign-minister level without preconditions, a reversal of its previous stand. For its part, Moscow has offered technical assistance in China's economic modernization.

Prospects

Obviously, other important factors exist whose future evolution will affect the nature of Sino-Soviet-Japanese relations. We do not know what the composition and outlook of the post-Brezhnev leadership will be. Countries outside the triangle can influence relationships within it. This is especially true of the United States. Domestic economic developments may constrain Soviet investment in Siberia; world market conditions may make foreign investment in this inhospitable and costly environment unprofitable. In Siberia and elsewhere, however, at least a possible alternative exists to the triangle of tension that has traditionally pitted Russia, China, and Japan in three-way confrontation and conflict. Whether that alternative becomes reality may depend as much on how leaders in these three countries perceive one another as on the objective merits of economic cooperation in an era in which exchanges of capital, technology, and natural resources seem destined to loom larger in the calculus of international politics.

Further Reading

Conolly, Violet. *Siberia Today and Tomorrow*. New York: Taplinger, 1976.

Jensen, Robert G., ed., *Conference on Soviet Natural Resources in the World Economy, 1980*. Washington, D.C.: Association of American Geographers, 1980.

Shabad, Theodore, and Victor L. Mote. *Gateway to Siberian Resources (The BAM)*. New York: Columbia University Press, 1969.

7/20
China

4

China's Food Prospects and Import Needs

A. Doak Barnett

From a global perspective, China, along with the United States and the Soviet Union, is one of the three key nations in the world food system. These three are the largest producers of food – including that most basic of all staples, grain – in the world.

The critically important roles played by the United States and the Soviet Union in global food supplies are widely known. The United States is by far the world's largest food exporter, meeting a huge proportion of the growing demand for grain in food-deficit countries; U.S. exports, in fact, dominate the world's grain trade even more than Saudi Arabian petroleum sales dominate the world's oil trade.

The Soviet Union is the world's largest unpredictable importer of grain. Because of several factors – including its highly variable weather and inefficiencies in its economic system – the Soviet Union's grain imports in recent years have fluctuated enormously, from close to zero to between 20 and 30 million metric tons (hereafter, tons) a year. These huge variations have been a major cause of instability – and dramatic price rises – in the world grain market, producing serious international consequences.

It is much less widely recognized that China is also unquestionably one of the most important countries in the world food system. First, it is one of the world's three largest producers of grain, accounting in recent years for about 36 percent of world output for rice, about 12 percent for wheat, and about 11 percent for coarse grain. Second, it feeds more people than any other nation – roughly 23 percent of the entire world population. And third, it plays a much more important role in the world's grain trade than is generally realized.

In recent years, China has been the largest importer of grain among developing nations. In 1978-1979, it imported more wheat than any other nation, developed or developing (and in 1979-1980, it was second only to the U.S.S.R.). At the same time, it has, in recent years, exported a substantial amount of rice, averaging about 1 million tons a year and generally accounting for between 10 and 20 percent of global rice trade; usually it is the second, third, or fourth largest rice exporter in the world. Furthermore, China's role in the world's grain trade is growing and will probably continue to do so in the period ahead. Rising Chinese imports of grain, which now include sizable amounts of coarse grains as well as wheat, will link China increasingly, in the context of the world food system, to its main suppliers – the United States, Canada, and Australia (and, to a lesser extent, Argentina).

A careful assessment of China's agricultural performance during the past three decades of communist rule reveals both successes and failures; any judgment on the balance sheet depends on one's perspective or the standards applied. In some respects, Chinese accomplishments have been impressive. During the quarter century between 1952 and 1977, the average rate of increase in China's grain output was more than 2 percent, about double the rate achieved during the previous fifty to a hundred years and about four times the long-term rate since the late fourteenth century. This rate, however, was somewhat below the worldwide average in developing countries during the period from the mid-1950s to the mid-1970s. More important, it was only marginally above the rate of growth in China's population during the same period.

Feeding the country's huge and growing population has been a notable achievement, but China's leaders have not been able to improve the population's diet during this period. It is true that there has been no known large-scale famine in China and that minimal nutrition standards have been maintained fairly equitably (through government control and rationing), at least for the majority of the population, ever since the disastrous years of the early 1960s, after the Great Leap Forward, when there was widespread and serious malnutrition. But China's new pragmatic leaders frankly admit that per capita grain supplies today are roughly what they were in the 1950s and that as many as 100 million Chinese are still inadequately fed.

China's food prospects for the 1980s involve many uncertainties. Output of grain and other agricultural products will certainly continue to rise, but so too will food demand; and the tension between supply and demand doubtless will continue and could become very serious.

Beijing's leaders now give agriculture extremely high priority in their overall development program, and they have adopted a wide variety of policies designed to spur output. They began to make agriculture a priority in the early 1960s. At that time they retreated from their original commune concept, restored "free plots" and "free markets," and adopted some other policies to increase peasant incentives. From then on, efforts were greatly increased to provide more modern inputs (such as chemical fertilizers) into agriculture, to start mechanization, and to improve water supplies and water control. Overall, however, in the 1960s and early 1970s, there were no dramatic increases in the proportion of state investment going directly to agriculture or to improvements in the agricultural system's organizational and incentive structures.

In the late 1960s and early 1970s, the average rate of increase in China's grain output rose to more than 3 percent, but in the early 1970s it fluctuated greatly and then, during 1975-1976, it stagnated. When the Maoist era ended with the chairman's death in 1976, China's grain supply, measured in per capita terms, was still roughly what it had been two decades earlier in the 1950s (although there had been some improvement in supplies of vegetables and certain other subsidiary foods).

With the inauguration of a new and extremely ambitious modernization program in 1978, Beijing's leaders raised even higher the priority of agriculture in their overall plans. In 1978, they announced an extraordinary grain output target for 1985: 400 million tons (compared to 283 million in 1977), requiring an average annual rate of increase of 4 to 5 percent—far above past average rates. This was clearly an unrealistic goal, and since the regime's "readjustment" in mid-1979, targets have been scaled down to more realistic levels. Nevertheless, Beijing has stepped up its investments in agriculture and has adopted many new policies that will help to speed agricultural modernization and increase output. In 1978, investment in agriculture accounted for only 10.7 percent of all central state investments; the plan for 1979 raised this to 14 percent, and further increases were called for in the future.

Equally important, during 1978-1980, the Chinese regime moved rapidly to adopt many new policies designed to alter the entire economy, including agriculture, in important ways, giving new emphasis to "material incentives," local initiative or autonomy, and "market forces." Beijing raised the state's purchase prices for major agricultural crops fairly dramatically (with some inflationary side effects in the cities). It granted greater authority to the communes' small production teams. And it permitted a substantial expansion of "private plots" and rural "free markets."

During 1978-1979, grain output soared, although the precise

reasons are difficult to identify. In 1978, production jumped 7.8 percent to 305 million tons. In 1979, it soared again. (There is some question, however, about whether or not some of the increase was statistical, that is, resulting from better statistical coverage.) In the spring of 1980, a top Beijing official said that 1979 output had been about 325 million tons; less than a month later, however, the State Statistical Bureau declared that it had been 332 million tons, almost 9 percent more than in 1978. Whichever of these figures is correct, the rise was impressive. Probably a large part of the explanation was good weather, the major cause of large year-to-year fluctuations in agricultural output in China or elsewhere. Beijing's new incentive policies must also have had important favorable effects. Such rates are not sustainable, however, and the target set by Beijing for grain output in 1980 was much lower—somewhat more than 3 percent.

There is no question that most of the new Chinese policies toward agriculture are sensible and should support future agricultural growth. But how rapidly China will actually be able to increase output not only of grain but also of other needed products remains to be seen. Ironically, the problem of raising production now is in a fundamental sense more difficult in China than it is in most developing countries, because Chinese agriculture is already highly developed, with per acre yields far above those in most developing nations. There is scope for much future growth—China's per acre yields are still well below those in many developed countries—but achieving this growth will not be easy.

China's shortage of arable land is its most fundamental problem. Most good arable land is already cultivated. Actually, during the past two decades, cultivated land has decreased from perhaps 107 million hectares to less than 100 million because land has been diverted to industrial and other uses. Present plans call for efforts to expand cultivated land again, but the potential for doing so will be limited at best and the process will be costly.

Present plans also call for greater diversification of crops and increased specialization in different areas of the country. This should contribute to productivity—and to meeting China's increasing needs for industrial and export crops as well as grain. But it may also result in less land being devoted to grain.

Better irrigation and water control are also planned. China, however, already has more of its cultivated land irrigated than any other large country in the world. Probably half of all its arable land is now under irrigation of some sort. Although Beijing plans to expand the amount of land under irrigation—and also to improve control of water on existing irrigated land—the process may be difficult and slow. Some major projects to divert Yangze River water to the North China plain (the agricultural area most in need of more water) are being seriously discussed, and in the long run they could be extremely important. But they are likely to take decades to build.

One of the important factors that has helped to raise yields in China during recent years has been the great increase in the use of modern fertilizers; starting in the 1960s, the Chinese rapidly increased their use of chemical fertilizers—especially nitrogen, from both domestic production and imports. This has been the main explanation for much of the yield increase they have achieved in recent years. Today, China is the fourth largest producer of chemical fertilizers in the world, and in recent years it also has been the world's largest importer of such fertilizers. By 1979, China supplied an average of well over 100 kilograms of chemical fertilizers (plus perhaps between 50 to 75 kilograms of organic fertilizers) to each cultivated hectare. Already, therefore, China is far ahead of most developing nations in this respect. It can still do more, however, and its leaders plan to do so. China's per hectare application of fertilizer remains well below that of many other countries, including the Netherlands, Japan, North Korea, and others. Chinese planners also intend to encourage use of a better mix of fertilizers (involving more phosphates and potash). The potential in these areas is still great. It has limits, however, and involves costs. The more chemical fertilizer is used, the less the "yield response" per ton tends to be under most circumstances, and there are indications that the fertilizer yield decline already is under way in China.

The Chinese are also gradually mechanizing agriculture. Policy toward use of larger machines has fluctuated, however. In 1978, at the start of the new modernization program, great stress was placed on rapid mechanization, a costly process. This policy has already been modified, and the pace has been slowed. The emphasis is now on more gradual, selective mechanization.

Another area of agricultural modernization in which the Chinese have made substantial progress, especially since the early 1960s, is new seed development. China has already begun its "green revolution," and the amount of land sown with improved, higher-yield seeds—especially rice seeds—has grown substantially. But the country still has a long way to go in this respect, and much of the increase in yields in the next few years may well come from better seeds.

In brief, China started its recent agricultural development with a traditional system of agriculture that was already far more advanced than that found in most developing nations; it has made significant strides in many aspects of modernization in recent years; and it now gives high priority to more rapid modernization and has adopted many sensible policies to spur faster growth. However, China faces enormous built-in constraints – especially the shortage of land – and will find it difficult to achieve rapid results in raising yields further, in part because the country had already attained fairly high yield levels.

What China needs in the period ahead is a comprehensive program of sophisticated agricultural modernization, involving an optimal mix of investments, inputs, and incentives. This will be difficult to achieve, and China unfortunately still lacks an adequate number of highly skilled agricultural scientists and technicians. Although its excellent organization for agricultural extension services survived the Cultural Revolution, its institutions for advanced training and research, in agriculture as in other fields, were badly damaged during the decade from the mid-1960s to the mid-1970s, and a generation that could have been trained was lost. Great efforts are now being made to remedy this deficit and to catch up. More stress is now being placed on research and training, both at home and abroad, than ever before. But it will take time to produce the results that are urgently needed.

In light of all these facts, how rapidly is China's production of grain – which includes the country's most important agricultural crops – likely to grow in the period ahead? No one can be certain. Almost certainly, however, growth will be well below the 4 to 5 percent rate projected in 1978. In fact, it may well be only slightly above the country's long-term rates since the 1950s – that is, between 2 and 3 percent. The country will be doing extremely well to exceed a 3 percent rate. To accomplish this goal, China will need political stability, continuity of policy, and luck – that is, no prolonged periods of disastrous weather.

The other side of the picture is that food demand is likely to grow considerably more rapidly in the period ahead than in the past, as a result of the crucial role that the regime has now given to incentive policies to spur greater productivity throughout the urban as well as the rural sectors of the economy. Since the 1950s, per capita demand for food has been kept low by controls and deliberate discouragement of hope for immediate improvement in living standards. Now, to try to inject a new dynamism into the economic system, Beijing has raised hopes for real improvement in the average person's standard of living and has introduced many new kinds of economic incentives. This new line will inevitably lead to greater pressures for a better diet. One aspect of these raised expectations that could have a major impact on the country's grain needs is increased consumption of meat. Already, this practice is beginning in China, with special emphasis on pork and chicken but also some on mutton and beef. For example, China's stock of hogs increased over 6 percent in 1979 to almost 320 million (roughly one hog for every three persons), and its output of all meat rose by 24 percent to 10.6 million tons. But, if allowed to do so, meat demand will probably rise much higher. (Even with the large increase in 1979, per capita meat production still amounted to only about 24 pounds per person during the year.) Obviously, therefore, demand for feed grain could rise substantially.

China simply cannot afford to undergo a "meat revolution" similar to those already experienced in the major noncommunist industrial countries and that now under way in the U.S.S.R. Nevertheless, any significant increase in meat consumption will have a major impact on grain demand, because it takes much more grain to produce a specified number of consumable calories by the conversion of (feed) grain to meat than by direct grain consumption.

Ever since its post-Leap economic crisis, China has been a large grain importer. In fact, during the nineteen years starting with 1961, it imported more than 100 million tons of grain, an average of 5.64 million tons a year (or about 4.5 million tons a year net, taking into account its rice exports). Moreover, the level of its grain imports has risen significantly in recent years. From the start of the 1960s to the mid-1970s, the average, with ups and downs, was around 5 million tons a year. During 1975 and 1976, the level dropped to 3.5 million tons and 2 million tons, respectively. But then grain imports rose to almost 7 million tons in 1977, almost 9.5 million tons in 1978, and roughly 11 million tons in 1979. There is a very real possibility that, in the period ahead, they will rise toward 15 million tons; they could even reach the range of 15 to 20 million tons a year.

During much of the 1960s (after the 1959–1961 depression in China) and 1970s, China imported grain (around 5 million tons a year) mainly to meet certain special needs and problems, especially feeding key urban areas. From the mid-1960s to the mid-1970s, grain imports amounted to only 2 to 3 percent of China's domestic production. However, they accounted for a higher percentage—perhaps 5 to 10 percent—of "commercial" or "commodity" grain, that is, grain actually traded; and they may have been close to the amount of grain that crossed provincial boundaries in China. Most important, they supplied the bulk of grain needed by some of China's largest cities. Grain was imported because it relieved the strain on internal transport and reduced the amount of grain that the state had to obtain from the hard-pressed peasants to feed its cities.

These reasons for importing grain will continue, but in the future there will be additional reasons: to support the regime's new incentives policy and its agricultural diversification program (which will divert some land to other crops) and to help achieve the improvements that Beijing has promised in nutrition and living standards. China cannot afford to become basically dependent on the world food market for any large percentage of its food needs, as many other countries now are. Nevertheless, its grain imports are likely to become larger and increasingly important both to China and to the international community as a whole.

It is clearly in the interest of the international community to assist China in every way possible to modernize its agriculture, to raise domestic output of grain and other agricultural products, and to meet its food needs to the maximum extent possible. A serious Chinese failure in agriculture would be an enormous human tragedy, and humanitarian motives alone dictate efforts to ensure that it will not occur. But there are practical reasons, too, to help the Chinese succeed. Failure would contribute greatly to the likelihood of political instability in China, which probably would affect its external relations in ways that, though unpredictable, would in all likelihood reverse recent moderate trends.

Even if China's new agricultural policies succeed, however, the Chinese are likely to become much more involved in the world food system – and in international scientific, technical, and educational as well as commercial links – than at any time in the past. This could well lead to many kinds of new, constructive relationships between China and the international community, relationships that should be welcomed, indeed strongly encouraged. This involvement with the world food system could also pose some new problems, however, that will need to be faced forthrightly.

There is a clear need for measures to achieve greater stability and predictability in the world food system as a whole, to ensure adequate reserves to meet global needs in bad years, and to prevent sudden, major price fluctuations that can be disastrous for poor countries and that tend to feed inflation in the industrialized nations. Even now, it is essential to involve China in these efforts; as Chinese imports increase, it will become increasingly important to do so. Although China's grain output – and its imports – have not fluctuated as greatly as those of the Soviet Union, in the past they have undergone sizable year-to-year changes. As its imports increase, any such fluctuations or changes will have a large global impact.

One major international step – long debated but still not close to general acceptance – that would help greatly to increase the stability of the world food system would be the creation of a global "food reserve system," consisting of internationally supervised but nationally owned reserves. If such a system can be established, it will be extremely important to include China in it. Chinese membership would probably be essential for such a system to succeed, and membership would clearly be in China's interest. In the interim, while no such system exists, it would be highly desirable to conclude at least bilateral agreements that would introduce some measure of stability into grain trade with China – agreements similar to the one the United States now has with the Soviet Union, or to those China already has signed with Canada, Australia, and Argentina, but which the United States and China have not yet concluded or even discussed seriously.*

More broadly, international cooperation in the field of agriculture that involves China should be energetically promoted. Not only can the more technically advanced countries assist agricultural modernization in China in many ways, but increased knowledge of Chinese experience in agriculture and rural development can also be of great value to many other nations – to less successful developing nations especially but, in a variety of ways, to industrialized nations as well.

Further Reading

A detailed bibliography on world food problems and China's agriculture and food situation will be found in "China and the World Food System," in A. Doak Barnett, *China's Economy in Global Perspective* (Washington, D.C.: The Brookings Institution, 1981).

---

*In October 1980, the United States and China signed a four-year agreement that committed China to purchase 6 to 8 million tons of grain a year from the United States (mainly wheat but 15 to 20 percent of the total to be corn), with additional purchases possible by agreement.

8410
china

5

China's Population in Perspective

Chi-hsien Tuan

Before the seventeenth century, the population of China oscillated around 50 to 60 million. Sometimes it fell as low as 7 million, but it hardly ever rose above 80 million.[1] By 1651, the population was somewhere near 50 million.[2] It was 542 million in 1949. In 1980 the population was officially announced as 982 million[3] – twenty times what it was 330 years ago. In the last 30 years alone, the population increased more than 80 percent.

Today, there are 102 persons per square kilometer in China. If China keeps growing the way it has for the past thirty years, by the end of the twenty-first century it will have a population four times the world population today. This is impossible. China's population growth must be stopped one way or another.

Historical Background

The decision to control population growth was made in 1957 amid a most ambiguous situation. Advocates of birth control were attacked by the Party as enemies of the people, while Party leaders decided that population growth must be planned.[4] Contraceptive activities were started in, and were mainly confined to, a few metropolitan areas where the expertise necessary for such services was available.[5] It was not until 1964 that the planned birth campaign was extended to all urban areas, which then contained about 12 percent of the total population. Subsequently, the urban birthrate was cut in half in three years.[6] The countryside was only sporadically affected by the planned birth campaign. The decision to implement planned birth measures in all rural as well as urban areas was not made until 1971.[7]

I wish to thank Dr. Griffith Feeney, who read the manuscript, discussed it with me, and made valuable suggestions for communicating Chinese practices and ideas to English readers.

Equally important, a number of measures were taken to strengthen planned birth work. A Planned Birth Leadership Group, presided over by a vice-premier, an official above a cabinet minister, was established at the State Council level, and a Planned Birth Office was created to carry out day-to-day implementation of planned birth policy. In the meantime, branch planned birth offices were set up at each level – provincial, city, district, county, and commune – with personnel engaged full-time in implementing planned birth work. Every work unit, including factories, schools, stores, government offices, and so on, also had personnel responsible for planned birth tasks. In the brigade, the woman captain was invariably in charge of these activities. Hence, a staff was created at all levels of government, under a national organization responsible for planned birth work.

In 1973, a birth quota system was established.[8] Under this system, the higher governmental body formulates a target population growth rate and determines the birth quota required to meet that target. Quotas are allocated to subordinate levels of government until they reach the grassroots level. The work units at the grassroots level distribute the birth quota to fertile married couples who have no children and then, if the quota is not exceeded, to women whose first child is at least 4 years old. Only women who have been authorized by their work unit to have a child are entitled to do so.

As planned birth work gets well under way and passes into the stage of single-child family policy, many new problems arise that need both immediate attention and long-term consideration. In 1981, on the recommendation of the Planned Birth Leadership Group and Planned Birth Office, a Commission on Planned Birth was established as a permanent government body in charge of planned birth policy and work, policy making for problems related to planned birth, and population research.

Organization of Planned Birth Work

Planned birth implementation involves three principal organizations: the Planned Birth Office, the medical establishment, and the comprehensive Party leadership structure.

The Planned Birth Office is responsible for birth planning, birth quota allocation to its subordinate levels, and implementation and supervision of planned birth work. It regulates the supply of contraceptive materials and controls the planned birth budget.

The Chinese medical establishment has an ingenious way of meeting the vast demand for contraceptive supplies with limited resources and manpower. The technical strategy of China's planned birth work relies on contraceptive operations, including IUD insertion, vasoligation and tubal ligation, and induced abortion. Surgical contraception is stressed because of its immediate effectiveness and its reliability. But surgical contraception requires trained medical personnel, and medical personnel are scarce in China.

In 1980, on the average, every doctor of Western medicine provided contraceptive services to more than 200 fertile married women in addition to providing medical care to the normal workload of 2,200 patients.[9] To make matters worse, these doctors usually live in commune centers (where commune hospitals are located), in townships, or in cities. China's strategy for dealing with the heavy medical workload and lack of rural services is to combine scarce technical personnel with villagers possessing a rudimentary education into a system that can meet the rural demand for contraceptives. Here the barefoot doctors and other rural paramedical personnel play an important role in linking urban doctors with their rural clients.

There were 1.58 million barefoot doctors and 3.58 million rural health workers and midwives in 1979.[10] These paramedical personnel are connected with doctors in the commune and county hospitals by a referral system; they work under the doctor's guidance and supervision. China is trying to train a female barefoot doctor who specializes in contraception in every brigade. The person in charge of contraception prepares for the visit of the well-trained doctors, who are organized into roving medical teams. Sometimes contraceptive-operation shock brigades tour the countryside, where they do IUD insertions with the help of the local barefoot doctors. The latter's constant on-the-spot care and follow-up services have made it possible for the better-trained doctors to serve more clients in wider areas. Today, many barefoot doctors have learned to insert and remove IUDs, and they arrange for abortions and sterilizations to be performed in hospitals. Through this arrangement, China possesses a great capacity for surgical contraception. In 1979, 31 million contraceptive operations and abortions were performed.[11]

The Party plays the most important role in the birth control campaign. The fact that planned birth involves every reproductive person's active participation requires not only that planned birth be observed by everyone, but more important, that it be promoted as an official Party program. This is a topic that cannot be explained in simple words. The following description roughly communicates the Chinese idea.

Ever since 1957, the situation in China has been such that people will take something seriously if it can be identified as a political task, and the authority to declare something "political" lies with the Party. Political authority is absolutely essential to the planned birth program because without it the program can simply be neglected. The decision to cut fertility is made not by the people themselves, but by the leadership. For the people to accept this decision, they must first be collected together by political authority to listen to the plan, then they must be convinced of the rationale of the decision, and finally, they must be induced to take action by example. After political authority has ensured people's participation, and education has convinced them of the necessity of planned birth, some of the cadres who are responsible for implementing the planned birth work exemplify the campaign by adopting contraceptive measures first. This helps drive away the people's unfounded fears, so that they will follow the example and adopt contraception. After planned birth has started, the Party does not withdraw, but remains in the background and watches over the work to ensure that it continues to progress.

Evolution of the Single-Child Family Policy

When planned birth first started in the early 1960s, a slogan offering a choice but indicating a preference came out in the propaganda: "One is best. Two square the account. Three is a mistake." By the mid-1970s, when planned birth was in full swing all over the land, the slogan was rephrased and became more stringent: "One is best. Two is the limit. Three is unacceptable." Later, detailed measures were outlined in three catchy words: "Wan (late marriage), Xi (spacing out), Shao (few births)." But since 1979, the single-child family policy has been put into practice and the criterion "one is best" has finally become the target for implementation.

By 1978, China's total fertility rate had been brought down to 2.3.[12] Still, a decision had to be made to cut fertility further. As China then had an annual natural increase of more than 12 million, it was considered necessary that a zero growth rate should be reached as soon as possible. Thus the single-child family policy, under which each couple is allowed to have only one child, was ushered in.

Preparation was made in 1979 to legislate planned birth into law,[13] but opinions differed, and no consensus regarding the single-child target was reached in 1980. Although Beijing fell into dispute over the proposed planned birth law, Guangdong Province took the lead by legislating a provincial planned birth ordinance, and all the other provinces implemented the single-child family policy by drawing up some provisional regulations. On February 13, 1980, the ordinance was promulgated.[14] The Guangdong Code may be a good reflection of general measures of implementing planned birth.

The major feature of the code is its use of economic incentive and disincentive as well as penalties as means of implementing planned birth; before, only political mobilization had been employed. The code was introduced essentially to induce the adoption of single-child families. Benefits, rewards, and special privileges from cradle to grave are so favorable that it seems the Chinese government means to "buy" people for the single-child family. The monthly allowance for those who agree to have only one child is about 10 percent of a worker's or peasant's usual income. In addition, there is favorable treatment for the single child ranging from health care to employment. Parents of a single child are given preference in allocations for living quarters in urban areas and in house-building foundations as well as in private plots in rural areas. Prolonged paid maternal leave and rewards are given to single-child mothers, and paid leave and rewards are given to women who undergo contraceptive operations. On the other hand, couples who have broken their promise to have only one child and have a second child must reimburse the government for all the benefits they have received, must pay higher prices for most—if not all—the goods and services necessary to rear a child, and lose their chances of promotion. Couples who go on to have a third child have to pay, among other things, a penalty of from 10 percent to 30 percent of their income.

Although the single-child family policy has not been legislated as a national code, it has been put into practice since 1979. The policy has received prestige and authority from an unusual "Open Letter"[15] issued by the Party on September 25, 1980, to its members and members of the Youth League, asking them to respond to the state's call to bear only one child.

The single-child family policy has rendered all the measures governing late marriage, late procreation, and child spacing unimportant. Marriage age is becoming less relevant to fertility, and restrictions on marriage age will gradually lose their significance as a means of birth control; child spacing is inapplicable when families are limited to one child. "One is best" has become the only criterion for fertility control.

Before discussing the rationale of the single-child family, one more point worth mentioning concerns legislation passed recently that is related to planned birth. Since 1978, planned birth has been covered by several laws. The 1978 Constitution of China stipulates that "the State promotes and carries out planned birth" (Article 53). In the Second Marriage Law, passed in 1980, it is stipulated that both the husband and wife "shall practice planned birth." The law defines marriage age as 22 for men and 20 for women, but these are considerably lower than the actual marriage age today. The law states that "late marriage and late procreation are encouraged."

The single-child policy is important not only because of its extraordinarily low target of fertility, but also because it has been put into practice by the world's most populous country. Therefore the rationale behind the policy is interesting. The policy was derived from a study made by Professors Song Gian, Wan Wanchen, Yu Jingyuan and Li Guangyuan, who built up a model to describe the population process and developed a theory called "best control program of population development" to give guidance as to the most desirable course of action. They projected the Chinese population[16] for 100 years (up to 2080) on different fertility levels as shown in Table 5.1. If final family

Table 5.1.   100-year projection of China's population (in billions)

Year	1.0	1.5	2.0	2.3 (1978 level)	2.5	3.0 (1975 level)
	(1)	(2)	(3)	(4)	(5)	(6)
1980	.978	.978	.978	.980	.983	.985
1985	1.002	1.009	1.024	1.041	1.052	1.069
1990	1.021	1.043	1.083	1.115	1.136	1.175
1995	1.037	1.086	1.152	1.201	1.231	1.297
2000	1.050	1.125	1.217	1.282	1.323	1.415
2005	1.054	1.151	1.267	1.349	1.400	1.520
2010	1.045	1.162	1.304	1.407	1.472	1.628
2015	1.026	1.166	1.339	1.467	1.551	1.754
2020	1.003	1.169	1.379	1.538	1.641	1.902
2025	.978	1.172	1.422	1.611	1.736	2.061
2030	.951	1.171	1.460	1.681	1.828	2.219
2035	.919	1.164	1.490	1.742	1.913	2.376
2040	.879	1.149	1.509	1.797	1.995	2.543
2045	.826	1.114	1.519	1.847	2.075	2.722
2050	.771	1.082	1.532	1.903	2.164	2.923
2055	.701	1.034	1.530	1.945	2.241	3.120
2060	.613	.967	1.507	1.968	2.300	3.309
2065	.523	.897	1.481	1.989	2.360	3.510
2070	.458	.849	1.478	2.036	2.448	3.757
2075	.407	.815	1.475	2.083	2.536	4.010
2080	.370	.777	1.472	2.119	2.614	4.264

Family size (Number of children per family)

Source: Song Jian et al., "Projection and Control of the Development
          of Population Process," System Engineering and Scientific
          Management, no. 2 (1980).

size (i.e., number of children per family) is set at 3, the population would grow to 1.4 billion in 2000. Any final family size above replacement level would result in growing population. If final family size is set at 2, a level slightly below replacement, the population would keep on growing and reach 1.2 billion in the next twenty years. With final family size at 1.5, the population would go on growing for forty-five years and reach a maximum of 1.17 billion in 2025 before it begins to decline. Even with a final family size of 1, i.e., the single-child family policy, population momentum would keep the population growing for another twenty-five years before it hit a maximum of 1.05 billion in 2005.

After examining these projections, Song and his collaborators came upon a plan named the U-shaped population control program.[17] The idea is that fertility must be rapidly brought down to a very low level and kept at a low level for a period to be decided by calculation, then raised to the replacement level. According to Song and his colleagues, this is the best way to bypass growth momentum.

Generally, conditions necessary for setting the target for the final family size are:

1. Within a certain period, the maximum population must be the lowest for all the possible programs;
2. Final family size must be a whole number not lower than 1;
3. The dependency ratio, i.e., the number of old (women over 60 and men over 65) and young (under 18) people compared to the number of people in the labor force (men aged 18–65 and women aged 18–60), must not go higher than a certain level;
4. The aging coefficient (i.e., the ratio between the mean age of the population and life expectancy at birth)[18] must not exceed a certain level.

That the target family size be a whole number (condition 2) is a matter of equality; the birth target assigned to each individual should be the same.

The population projection based on one child per family for the next twenty-five years meets with the above conditions. The details are shown in Tables 5.1 and 5.2.

Table 5.1 shows, first of all, that the maximum population based on the single-child family is less than that for all the other fertility levels. It also shows that under this policy the maximum size will be reached in the shortest time; under the other policies it will take longer before population begins to decline. That is, this program would bring the population to a stable state soonest.

Table 5.2. China's projected population situation according to the single-child family policy

Year	(Aging coefficient) (1)	Ratio of old to young (2)	Dependency Ratio (3)	Number in labor force (100 million) (4)	Average age of the population (5)
1980	0.39	0.16	0.89	5.2	26.8
1985	0.42	0.22	0.67	6.1	29.1
1990	0.46	0.34	0.48	6.9	31.7
1995	0.48	0.48	0.40	7.4	33.8
2000	0.51	0.62	0.38	7.6	35.9
2005	0.54	0.72	0.40	7.5	38.0
2010	0.57	0.92	0.42	7.4	40.5
2015	0.60	1.3	0.44	7.1	43.2
2020	0.63	1.9	0.48	6.8	45.7
2025	0.67	2.6	0.56	6.3	48.5
2030	0.70	3.6	0.72	5.5	51.0

Source: See Table 5.1.

The dependency ratio in 1981 is 0.9 (See Table 5.2). By the year 2005 it would be as low as 0.4. The labor force would be at its maximum of 760 million in the year 2000 – 240 million higher than in 1981.

After 2005, fertility should be raised to the replacement level. This would complete the U-shaped course of fertility control, and the population would avoid the consequences of a peaky age distribution. This policy leads the population to a manageable situation from which it can experience decline. The Chinese hope to settle the size at around 700 million.

Contraceptive Achievement and Birth Decline

One question remains: How effective is the planned birth policy? As the birth campaign started to cover all rural areas only in the 1970s, birth rates for the decade (see Table 5.3) may give us some idea of the recent results. In 1970, the birthrate was 33.6 per 1,000 population. It was 17.9 about ten years later, a 47 percent decline. But people outside China are usually skeptical about Chinese statistics. A recent instance is provided by Banister and Preston, who claimed that China's mortality statistics were only 80–90 percent complete throughout the 1970s.[19] Even if this were applied uncritically to birth registration, it would not affect the fact that the birth rate was cut almost in half in the 1970s.

There are other ways to test the reliability of the birth rates in Table 5.3. For example, 1975 and 1978 age distributions show that the number of births has been declining substantially. But there is other information, independent of vital registration, to show the decline in the birthrate. These are the statistics of contraceptive operations, which have become available only recently. Table 5.4 gives estimates of rates of contraceptive use based on these data.[20] The data should be reliable because they are the basis on which the Health Department and hospitals ask for reimbursement from the Planned Birth Offices.

It must be noted that the rate refers to women between ages 24 and 44. Age 24 is used in practice because the minimum age at marriage is 23, and 24 is about the average marriage age of rural women. It is hoped that the rate for this group will be as close as possible to that for all married women of reproductive age, as marriage is universal in China.

Table 5.4 shows that in 1979 almost three-fourths of Chinese women of reproductive age were involved in contraception programs. In the same year there were 18 million births that might have engaged

Table 5.3. China: Crude birthrate 1970-1979

Year	No. of live births per 1000 population	Natural increase per 1000 population	Expected birthrate (no. of births expected per 1000 population)
	(1)	(2)	(3)
1970	33.6	26.0	--
1971	30.7	23.4	35
1972	29.9	22.3	32
1973	28.1	20.9	27
1974	25.0	17.6	23
1975	23.1	15.8	18
1976	20.0	12.7	18
1977	19.0	12.1	18
1978	18.3	12.0	17
1979	17.9	11.7	17

Source: For columns 1 and 2 see Liu Zheng, "The Present Situation and the Development of China's Population," paper presented at the Beijing International Round Table Conference on Demography, 1980. Column 3 was calculated using the formula Y = 45.4 - 38X, where Y is birth-rate and X is rate of use of contraception. See Dorothy L. Nortman and Ellen Hofstatter, Population and Family Planning Programs, 9th ed. (New York: Population Council, n.d.).

Table 5.4. China: Current rate of use of contraception, 1971-1979

Percentage of women age 24-44 who currently practice contraception

Year	Total .	Rate of use of measures other than sterilization	Sterilization rate		
			Total	Tubal ligation	Vasoligation
	(1)	(2)	(3)	(4)	(5)
1971	27	24	3	2	1
1972	36	30	6	3	3
1973	48	37	10	6	4
1974	59	46	13	8	5
1975	71	53	18	10	8
1976	72	52	20	12	8
1977	73	49	24	14	10
1978	74	47	27	15	12
1979	74	43	31	18	13

Source: Estimated mainly according to Zhang Lizhong, "Birth Control, Late Marriage and the Decline of Population Growth Rate," Renkou Yu Jingyi, No. 1, 1980. For 1978 and 1979, estimation is based on data given by Jian Kang Bao, January 27, 1980, and September 9, 1980, respectively.

27 percent of fertile women in reproduction; this seems to indicate that all women without a birth permit were practicing birth control. As China relies chiefly on surgical contraception (i.e., IUDs and sterilization), column 2 in Table 5.4 actually reflects the current rate of use of IUDs, the major means of birth control in China. The rate of use of IUDs started at 24 percent in 1971 and went quickly up to more than 50 percent of fertile women; after 1976 it dropped down to 43 percent. But the sterilization rate increases all the time, and by 1979 more than 30 percent of fertile couples were sterilized either by tubal ligation or vasoligation.

The question remains: How well do the rates of use agree with the birth decline? To answer the question, Nortman and Hofstatter's formula[21] is used to derive the expected birthrate from the rate of use of contraceptives and crude birthrate; expected birthrates are shown in column 3 of Table 5.3. The expected birthrates and the observed birthrates agree quite well, especially in recent years. This consistency of rates of use of contraceptives with the observed birthrates lends credibility to both series.

The above illustration is consistent with China's rapid birth decline. In the 1960s, the total fertility rate may have been near 5.[22] Song and his group have also demonstrated that the total fertility rate was 3 for 1975, 2.6 for 1976, 2.4 for 1977, 2.3 for 1978,[23] and 2.2 for 1979.[24] In the 1970s, the total fertility rate may have declined 56 percent, against 47 percent for the crude birthrate. Before 1949 women used to marry at the early age of about 18; now rural women are believed to marry after age 24. Abortion is widely practiced. In the 1970s, the ratio of live births to abortions was 4:1.[25] There are other measures that delay procreation. Combining all the effects of contraception, late marriage, late procreation, child spacing, induced abortions, and so on, a halving of the 1970 birthrate in ten years is not improbable. Then does this achievement justify the statement that China's planned birth program works remarkably well?

Conclusion

The single-child family policy has become a most important phenomenon and will have profound consequences for every aspect of Chinese life for many years to come. It has naturally created worries and concerns within as well as without the country. Ansley Coale has examined the situation and arrived at this conclusion: "Because fertility was not reduced in the 1950s and 1960s, . . . positive growth must be accepted into the next century. Neither the extremely low fertility required to stop growth by 2000, nor the subsequent extremely unbalanced age distribution are acceptable as practical goals of policy."[26] In the summer of 1980 he made his argument known to a Beijing audience that ranged from university teachers of demography to China's population policy maker, Vice-Premier Chen Muhua. But the Chinese are resolute in pursuing the single-child family, for they think Song's U-shaped program will guard them from these dangers. (See Table 5.2, especially the dependency ratio in column 3.)

The worry over age structure is well founded. But it must be noted as well that the problem of size has become paramount, and it must now be dealt with by any means. Limiting population size would entail costs in many aspects of society; the highest one may be the unbalanced age structure. But balancing age structure would result in a faster population growth, one that is far more expensive than the society can bear. The sensible idea is to harmonize the two, with stress on size, so that the gain from limiting size outweighs the burden from an unbalanced age distribution. It is this goal that the U-shaped program aims to achieve.

The single-child policy may prove to be unrealizable. But there is no harm in making it the ideal target. Doing as much as possible to bring fertility down and maintaining fertility at a low level before it is raised to replacement level—this is what the Chinese are doing. While China is making energetic efforts to implement the single-child policy, it is also prepared to deal with a population size of 1.2 billion by 2000, which may happen if the total fertility rate cannot be brought down below 2.

But the real trouble does not lie merely on the economic side. Although Song's projection is able to answer some important economic questions, it cannot answer all the questions, for the single-child policy is really a revolution that not only challenges the major aspects of the present order of life, but would bring about problems that have not yet surfaced. These problems are mostly social, cultural, and psychological. The economic advantages of the policy are generally foreseeable, but its disadvantages in other areas are still unknown. Warnings about the problems of caring for the old should be dealt with seriously. It is courageous enough for China to seek the advantage of the smallest possible population, yet it may not be superfluous to consider what the ill consequences might be and how they should best be met. China has gone very far and installed population control as its major goal. This demands full attention from society. Single-child policy must be an integral part of all government development plans. Population must accordingly be fixed, by legislation if necessary, as the common denominator of all government work and planning.

Notes

1. From Xie Zhongliang, "China's Historical Population Statistics," in *Treatises on Population Problems*, a publication of the Journal of Sichuan University, no. 3, 1979 (in Chinese).

2. From Zhou Yuanhe, "Analyzing the Dubious Points on Population Figures in the Early Qing Dynasty," *Fudan Journal*, no. 3, 1980, p. 26 (in Chinese).

3. From *Ta Kung Bao* (American Edition), May 2, 1981 (in Chinese).

4. The exact time of this decision remained unsettled until 1980 when Lo Qing, in the preface to a book *What Population Studies Do*, (a collection of papers published in the 1950s by scholars advocating birth control, reprinted (in Chinese) by the Chinese Sociology Association in 1980) wrote, "In February 1957, Chairman Mao, at the Supreme Conference of State Affairs, accepted the proposal by Shao Lizi, Ma Yinchu and Tao Menghe on birth control and late marriage, and decided to establish a commission on population studies and an institute of population research." Although neither was set up then, Lo stated definitely that "this was the wise strategical decision made by our Party." For further information, see *Selected Works of Mao Zedong* (1977), Vol. 5, p. 488, and *Mao Zedong Sixiang Wansui* [Long live Mao Zedong thought] (n.d.), pp. 97, 107, 143, and 156 (in Chinese).

5. The birthrate in metropolitan areas like Beijing was found to be declining in 1958. See Ling Ruizhy, "A Brief Account of 30 Years' Mortality of Chinese Population," paper presented at WHO/ESCAP meeting on Mortality in Asia, 1980, Manila.

6. See Liu Zheng, "The Present Situation and the Development of China's Population," paper presented at the Beijing International Round Table Conference on Demography, 1980.

7. This was well known in China as State Council Directive No. 51. See Pichao Chen, "The Birth Planning Program," paper presented at the China Population Analysis conference at the East-West Population Institute, East-West Center, Honolulu, 1980.

8. See *Renkou Lilun* [Population theory] (Commercial Press, 1977), p. 134. A part of this book is translated by H. Yuan Tien in his book *Population Theory in China* (White Plains, N.Y.: M. E. Sharpe, 1980).

9. Calculations are based on 1980 statistics officially released by the State Bureau of Statistics. See *Ta Kung Bao* (American edition), May 2, 1981 (in Chinese).

10. See *Zhongguo Baike Nian Jian* (Beijing, 1980), p. 561 (in Chinese).

11. From *Jian Kang Bao* [Health news], September 9, 1980 (in Chinese).

12. This was disclosed by China's Minister of Health Chien Xingzhong; see *Jian Kang Bao* [Health news], September 11, 1980 (in Chinese).

13. See Vice-Premier Chen Muhua's report at the 1979 Session of the People's Congress, "Realization of Four Modernizations Hinged on Planned Control of Population Growth." *People's Daily*, August 11, 1979 (in Chinese).

14. For the full text, see *Nangfang Ribao*, February 13, 1980 (my translation).

15. See *People's Daily*, September 25, 1980 (in Chinese).

16. See Song Jian, Wan Wanchen, Yu Jingyuan, and Li Guangyuan, "Projection and Control of the Development of Population Process," *System Engineering and Scientific Management*, no. 2, 1980 (in Chinese).

17. Although the specific program for China may be U-shaped, in other cases it may not be; the U-shape implies that the beginning fertility level is the same as the final fertility level. Oftentimes, the latter would be lower, forming a J-shaped schedule.

18. Aging coefficient is defined as the ratio of the mean age of a population to its life expectancy at birth. When the aging coefficient is 1, the population is very old; it is young when the coefficient is very small. Population aging is moderate if the aging coefficient has a value near ½.

19. Judith Banister and Samuel H. Preston, "Mortality in China," *Population and Development Review*, Vol. 7, no. 1 (1981).

20. Interested readers may refer to my forthcoming paper, "China's Population and Planned Birth."

21. See Dorothy L. Nortman and Ellen Hofstatter, *Population and Family Planning Programs*, 9th ed. (New York: Population Council, n.d.), p. 90.

22. Zhou Guangfu reported in his article "Single-Child Policy Is the Best Way to Level Off the Effect of Birth Peaks," *Treatises on Population Problems, Journal of Sichuan University*, no. 3, 1979 (in Chinese), that according to a survey in Hunan Province, the mean number of children ever born per married woman was 4.2 (1950s), 4.9 (1960s), and 2.9 (1970s).

23. Song Jian et al., "Projection and Control."

24. Chen Muhua, "Realizations of Four Modernizations."

25. Estimated from information given in Song Jian et al., "Projection and Control."

26. See Ansley J. Coale, "Population Trends, Population Policy and Population Studies in China," *Population and Development Review*, Vol. 7, no. 1 (1981).

7230

China,

6

China's Role in the Energy Development of Asia and the Pacific: The Next Twenty Years

Kim Woodard

A brief review of the basic conditions affecting energy development in the Asia-Pacific region is in order before we can be in a position to describe the current state of the Chinese energy system, the probable course of its development over the next twenty years, and the relationship of that development to the other countries of the region.

Energy in the Asia-Pacific region is characterized first of all by an unevenness of consumption. A single country, Japan, consumes fully a third of the commercial energy commodities available in the region. China consumes another third. The other countries split the rest. Per capita annual commercial energy consumption varies between Japan's average level, 4,000 kilograms coal equivalent, and the average in Asian developing countries, about 300 kilograms coal equivalent. In other words, disparities in energy living standards around the region are at least an order of magnitude. Low levels of energy consumption, compared to developed countries, are of course not atypical of the Third World generally.

Asian energy systems have a second characteristic in common with energy systems in other Third World regions, namely a heavy dependence on imported petroleum to satisfy the demands of the modern sectors of the region's developing countries. But Asian developing countries are modernizing the industrial, transportation, and urban sectors of their economies at a faster rate, between 5 to 10 percent per year. This high growth rate for the modern sectors of Asian

Figures 6.1, 6.2, 6.3, 6.4, and 6.5 are reproduced from the author's book *The International Energy Relations of China* (Stanford, California: Stanford University Press, 1980) with the kind permission of Stanford University Press.

developing economies greatly accelerates the pace of development of the economy as a whole and can be viewed as a critical "engine of development" for the region. But rapid growth in the modern sectors has a secondary and less desirable effect: it accelerates the demand for imported petroleum to feed the furnaces of industry, the new forms of transportation, and the energy needs of the burgeoning cities. Unchecked growth in the modern sectors may also seriously damage the environment and severely strain the balance-of-payments and foreign-currency-reserves positions of countries throughout the region. On balance, however, the consequences of rapid growth in the modern sectors of Asian economies are widely accepted as necessary, even desirable, because of the special contribution these sectors make to general economic growth and eventually to individual living standards.

In the 1980s, Asia, along with the already industrialized regions of the world, faces a new and highly serious dilemma in the course of the energy transition. Many experts on the world petroleum market, including prominent U.S. government experts and some of my colleagues at the East-West Center, are suggesting that we are now entering what might be called the "plateau phase" of the world oil market. In the wake of the revolution in Iran and the subsequent international crisis in the Persian Gulf, some of the largest OPEC producers are setting long-range ceilings on petroleum production capacity, output, and exports. These ceilings are designed to conserve finite resources, to slow the torrent of surplus foreign exchange earnings, and to stabilize the price of crude petroleum at an extremely high level. The newer and smaller oil-exporting countries like Mexico and China, which face sharp resource and domestic-consumption constraints on their long-range export potential, cannot be expected to contribute more than a small amount to the world market. Their small increments are generally balanced by the slow decline of production capacity and exports in older producing countries like Venezuela and Indonesia. The net effect of all these changes may be to stabilize at current absolute levels the total volume of oil that is in trade on the world market. Hence, we are entering the plateau phase in the world market, just ten years after reaching a similar plateau in annual U.S. crude petroleum production. The experts continue to disagree about the advent of the plateau phase: Some project continued growth for a few years; others project an actual decline in world crude oil trade during the 1980s. Whatever the outcome of this debate, few would question the assertion that if we are not already in the plateau phase, we are likely to enter it in the not too distant future.

Whenever it arrives, a plateau in the world oil market is bound to have serious consequences for economic development throughout the Asia-Pacific region. The developing countries of the region that import oil cannot sustain 5 to 10 percent annual growth rates in their industrial, transportation, and urban sectors without continued increases in oil imports. They must, therefore, search for alternative large-scale commercial energy production technologies or face critical damage to the pace of development of their economies. They must conduct this search for alternative commercial energy technologies within a desperately short time frame and under serious limitations of capital and resources. They must also adapt alternative commercial energy production technologies under development in the industrial countries to a scale and level of technical complexity that fits comfortably into the framework of their domestic economies. Providing liquid fuels for the further development of transportation sectors may present particularly acute difficulties.

From my own observations of both energy development and political alignments within the Asia-Pacific region, I am increasingly driven to conclude that patterns of energy cooperation among clusters of countries within the region have tended to coincide with tacit regional security coalitions. In Asia and the Pacific, political alignment on security issues tends to occur in relatively subtle and hidden ways, especially in the wake of the protracted and disastrous war in Vietnam. I believe that we are witnessing the gradual emergence of at least three security clusters in the region. The first, the new triangular security coalition among China, Japan, and the United States, is perhaps the most visible. This security triangle is greatly reinforced by developing patterns of energy cooperation among the three partners in the coalition. The second tacit security coalition coincides with the Association of Southeast Asian Nations (ASEAN). Although ASEAN's functions are strictly limited to economic cooperation, the foreign ministers of the ASEAN countries now meet regularly to discuss such issues as Vietnam's expansion in Indochina and Soviet naval expansion in the Western Pacific. The third emergent Asia-Pacific security coalition is the political and security agreement between the Soviet Union and Vietnam, formalized in a treaty that has explicit military consultation clauses.

In the case of all three new coalitions, cooperation in energy development projects is a principal arena of collective action and exchange. Thus, more than a merely coincidental relationship appears to exist between energy and security cooperation throughout Asia and the Pacific. This interface between energy and security may have important implications for China's energy role in Asia, implications to which I will return.

China's Energy System in 1980

As of 1980, the People's Republic of China was already well down the road toward large-scale development of its commercial energy infrastructure. Here I can provide only a few brief glimpses of China's domestic energy system, sketching the general outlines of that system from a variety of perspectives.

In terms of basic energy resources, China must be considered among the best endowed countries in the world. Coal resources are extremely large, ranking with those of the United States and the Soviet Union at well over 1 trillion metric tons of recoverable bituminous coal. Measured and inferred coal reserves are now reported by the Chinese government at 600 billion metric tons, enough to provide for production at current levels for 1,000 years. The extent of China's crude petroleum and natural gas resources is still shrouded in uncertainty, both because of the early stage of exploration yet achieved and because of the reluctance of the Chinese government to reveal more than the most general information about its oil and gas discoveries. Foreign geologists place recoverable crude petroleum resources at about 10 billion metric tons, or 70 to 75 billion barrels. The U.S. Department of Energy uses a general figure of 100 billion barrels, a figure said to reflect China's internal estimates. A reasonable range of estimates for economically recoverable crude petroleum resources, including highly speculative estimates for the continental shelf, would be in the range of 10 to 20 billion metric tons, or 75 to 150 billion barrels. This would be a substantial endowment of petroleum resources that could meet China's domestic demand for petroleum over the coming decades with little difficulty. Even at the upper end of this range of oil and gas resource estimates, however, China would have less than half the recoverable oil and gas resources originally in place in U.S. fields. Thus, oil and gas resources represent a serious constraint on the overall pattern of development for the People's Republic, a constraint that will, among other things, sharply limit the amount of petroleum available for export.

China's hydropower resources, like its coal resources, are among the largest in the world. With 500 gigawatts of potential hydropower capacity, Beijing could run an electric power infrastructure comparable in size to the entire U.S. power grid, including thermally generated electricity, on hydropower alone. But there are also serious constraints on development of this enormous hydropower potential. Many of the largest potential sites are located in remote areas, far from consumption centers. For example, the Yalutsangpu River, which has the largest potential hydropower site in the world, is located high in the Himalayas, at an impossible distance from industrial centers. Long-distance high-voltage transmission technology is still being developed; it may someday provide a means of exploiting such distant hydropower potential. For the present, however, the development of such sites is not a viable alternative for China. There are, of course, many remaining sites available in the eastern portion of the country that could be developed for more immediate needs. Development of most of these sites, however, would entail the sacrifice of significant areas of cropland. In a country with four times the population of the United States and two-thirds the agricultural land area, the loss of prime agricultural land to hydropower development would be serious.

Little information is available outside China about the country's uranium resources. I would guess that reasonably assured uranium oxide (U_3O_8) resources that could be exploited at a cost of US \$30 to \$50 per kilogram are on the order of 100,000 metric tons, or about 20 percent of the comparable figure for North America. Annual production of yellowcake might be in the range of 1,000 to 2,000 metric tons per year, on the order of South African output. Currently produced uranium is stockpiled and used for weapons. China at present has no commercial nuclear power reactors, although there are strong indications that Beijing might import its first light-water reactor in the next few years, perhaps bringing it on line by 1985.

A close and traditional balance has existed between primary energy production and aggregate energy consumption in China during the postrevolutionary period. Even in the 1950s, China imported only about 3 percent of commercial energy consumption in the form of petroleum products from the Soviet Union. At present, about 2 to 3 percent of primary energy production is exported in the form of crude oil exports to Japan and other Asian countries. This equivalence between the production and consumption sides of the energy balance is a matter of deliberate and persistent official policy.

How impressive is China's record of energy development? If one does a careful comparison of its growth rates with those of other countries, the inescapable conclusion emerges that the People's Republic is expanding its commercial energy system at a pace not at all out of line with experience in other parts of the Third World. The average annual growth rate of primary energy production for China was 8.8 percent between 1961 and 1977. This figure, to be sure, is well above the world average growth rate of 5.1 percent per year during the same period. The average growth rate in the same period for all Third World areas excluding China, however, is 8.9 percent. This comparison is not entirely fair. For one thing, the average Third World energy production growth rate includes inflated figures for the petroleum industries of the Middle East and other oil-exporting countries. Another important factor in the equation is that China earns each additional increment of commercial energy consumption with an increment of domestic energy production, production which is fully owned and controlled by Beijing. The same statement could not be made of many areas of the Third World.

How advanced, efficient, and productive is China's energy production technology? This is a question subject to sharp debate among experts in various energy industries who have visited the People's Republic. The general consensus, however, is that China lags by one or two decades behind the most advanced Western countries in the level of technology available to its energy industries. Beijing is taking serious steps to compensate for this technical lag in its current ten-year development plan. The effort to catch up in energy technology includes reestablishment of important technical education centers and the funding of indigenous research and development programs. But the ten-year plan also includes a heavy dose of foreign technology acquisition.

The basic components of Chinese industry, including the energy industries, are produced by domestic machine-building factories. For example, China produces standard generators for its electric power plants, generally within defined limits on generator size and on the sophistication of the generating units themselves. In addition, a few experiments have been done with large and technically sophisticated generators in the 300-megawatt range, and periodic reports appear that a prototype 600-megawatt generator is under construction. On the whole, however, the large, sophisticated prototypes are intended more to advance the general level of Chinese technology in the field of generator manufacture than to provide a steady production stream of large, complex, and doubtless highly expensive units. The manufacture of basic refinery components, drilling equipment, coal mining equipment, and other energy production equipment is handled similarly; the government prefers to stick to the tried and true for the bulk of its effort.

This approach to domestic energy equipment manufacture is probably cost effective and avoids the design of units that are too large or too complicated for ready integration into the rest of the industrial production system. On the other hand, this strategy leaves a considerable gap between China and the rest of the world in the technological level of equipment produced. This gap is the origin of most of the negative foreign reports on the state of Chinese energy technology.

Beijing, of course, recognizes the limits of its own strategy of equipment design and manufacture. Basic domestically produced units are therefore supplemented by highly selective technology-import programs that provide a steady stream of the more advanced energy production technologies to areas of energy development, such as offshore development, that would be slowed or seriously impaired by total reliance on indigenous technology and equipment. As a rule, Beijing carefully balances expenditures on foreign energy equipment with trade income generated by the sale of crude petroleum, coal, and other energy commodities. In the years between 1972 and 1978, the amount spent on energy plant and equipment imports almost exactly balanced the amount earned from the export of energy commodities—both about US $4 billion. Beijing also carefully allocates its available energy plant and equipment purchases. It prefers West European and Japanese companies for well-established technology, such as refinery and petrochemical plants, and U.S. firms for "cutting-edge" energy technologies, such as seismic exploration and data-processing equipment, satellite remote sensing packages, or secondary recovery technology—all areas in which the United States retains a significant technological lead over its principal competitors.

We should not overemphasize the amount we know about the current state of the Chinese energy system. Much of the data on which foreign analysts base estimates is still subject to considerable doubt. The Chinese government is increasing the amount of statistical information it publishes on its energy system, but some of the data are internally inconsistent, raising doubts about its overall accuracy. In addition, for certain important energy parameters the Chinese government itself has no data whatsoever. For example, China, like many largely rural and agricultural societies, consumes a substantial proportion of its energy in the form of "noncommercial" or traditional fuels—firewood, animal waste, agricultural residues, and the like. But there are simply no data on the absolute or relative contribution of these traditional fuels to the Chinese energy economy beyond some rough order-of-magnitude estimates by foreign experts.

It is in the context of these serious gaps in information and basic knowledge that we must consider any effort to project the development of China's energy infrastructure into the future. Making any statement about the future is hazardous. Long-range projections are consequently directed more toward eliminating highly unlikely outcomes than toward establishing a precise range of estimates. And so with this word of caution I turn to the future of the Chinese energy balance.

Projecting China's Energy Future

At present, the People's Republic of China (PRC) already has the world's third-largest commercial energy infrastructure, even without taking into account the further increment of noncommercial energy provided by traditional fuels in the countryside. China consumes roughly as much energy each year as Japan, and China's primary energy production is equivalent to that of Saudi Arabia. The combination of a large energy production sector and a large consumption sector ranks the PRC third behind the United States and the Soviet Union, but the gap between China and the superpowers is still substantial. China produces about one third as much commercial energy as the Soviet Union and one fifth as much as the United States. However, my projections indicate that China may be able to close the larger part of this gap by the year 2000.

Let us glance for a moment at the structure of the energy balance projection model for China shown in Figure 6.1 before moving on to the substance of the projection findings. The model consists of three basic sectors. The production sector is driven by variable resource estimates for the oil and gas industries and variable capital investment rates for the electric power industry and the coal industry. The model cascades primary energy from resource discovery functions through primary and secondary production, eliminating various inefficiencies, nonenergy use, and waste, and provides inferential figures for energy availability from each of the domestic industries. The consumption side of the model is based on standard assumptions regarding variable rates of economic growth, population growth, and efficiencies of energy use, expressed in the form of energy/GNP regression coefficients. I treat net energy export potential as a residual category that drops out as the difference between the production and consumption of the model. The export potential figure thus represents a ceiling on the amount of energy that China could export under various resource and economic growth scenarios, not a projection of the absolute level of exports that is likely to occur within that ceiling. On the whole, the

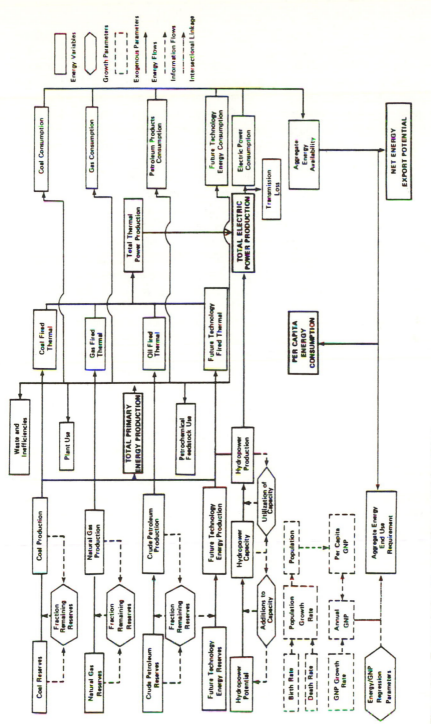

Figure 6.1 Energy balance projection model for China

model is based on standard energy modeling techniques and is relatively aggregate in nature. Tailored specifically to the Chinese case, it has a number of special features, such as variable discovery rates and decaying elasticity coefficients, that were introduced to handle the range of uncertainty in the Chinese data base.

The first projection (see Figure 6.2), intended to illustrate some of the dynamics of the model within relatively short time horizons, contains only a few of the variables in the model and is just one of the hundreds of scenarios produced in the course of working with the model. Note the top two curves, gently descending from left to right. These curves represent the slow depletion of recoverable oil and gas resources under a highly constrained set of resource and discovery assumptions. The middle curves represent annual oil and gas production, which rise, reach plateaus, and then begin to fall off toward the end of the century. Again, keep in mind that this is a pessimistic scenario. The solid hump-shaped curve on the bottom represents the introduction and then decline of net exports of energy commodities on a limited scale. Under the assumptions of this scenario, net exports would cross over into net imports by roughly the early 1990s. Meanwhile, limits on oil and gas resources would force Beijing to invest heavily in production from alternative technologies.

Figure 6.3 shows what would happen to Chinese oil and gas production under a wide range of resource assumptions. The lowest set of curves (R_1) shows the outcome if Meyerhoff and Willums (1976) are correct that China's crude oil resources are on the order of 10 billion metric tons, or 75 billion barrels of recoverable oil. Production would peak at nearly 200 million metric tons per year of crude petroleum and 200 billion cubic meters per year of natural gas during the 1990s, then would begin a long, slow decline. If this scenario seems to give rise to too rapid a peaking at too low a production level, keep in mind that Meyerhoff and Willums placed nearly half the projected discoveries in this set of resource estimates in the offshore theaters.

The oil and gas production curves represented by R_2 would occur if we were to double the Meyerhoff-Willums estimates of China's recoverable petroleum resources. This would give China an initial endowment of roughly 20 billion metric tons (150 billion barrels) of recoverable crude petroleum, about half of the recoverable oil and gas resources originally in place in the United States. Under this relatively optimistic set of resource assumptions, China's oil production would reach a plateau at the end of the century at about 300 million metric tons per year, or 6 million barrels per day.

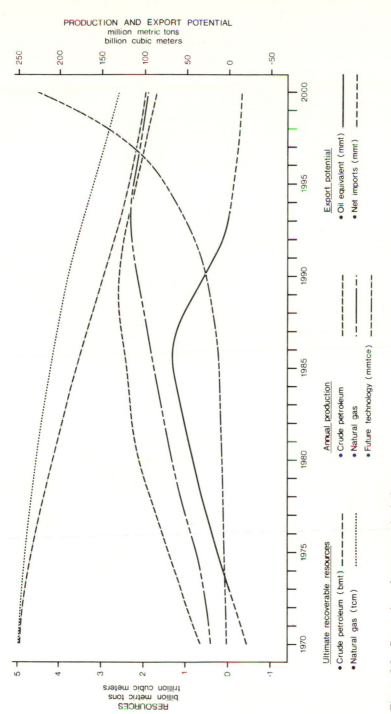

PRODUCTION AND EXPORT POTENTIAL
million metric tons
billion cubic meters

Annual production
• Crude petroleum
• Natural gas
• Future technology (mmtce)

Export potential
• Oil equivalent (mmt)
• Net imports (mmt)

Ultimate recoverable resources
• Crude petroleum (bmt)
• Natural gas (tcm)

RESOURCES
billion metric tons
trillion cubic meters

Figure 6.2 Dynamics of resource depletion

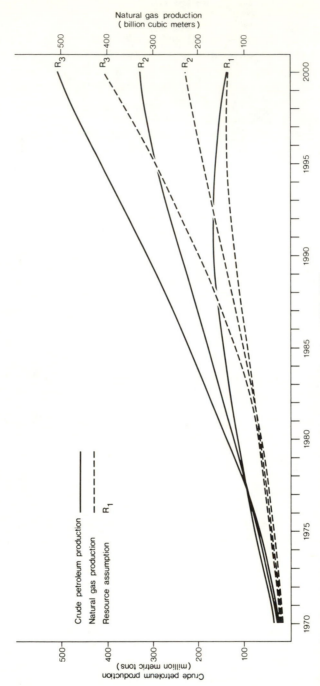

Figure 6.3 Projected crude petroleum and natural gas production, 1970–2000

The upper set of curves (R_3) shows what might happen if China hit an oil and gas bonanza either in the offshore theaters or in the far western sedimentary basins. Assuming the most favorable set of resource and capital allocation conditions, a quadrupling of the Meyerhoff-Willums resource estimates, and twenty years without significant political disruption of the oil and gas industries, China would become one of the world's largest producers by the end of the century. This is the scenario resulting from various optimistic assessments of China's oil and gas potential. I do not consider it a highly likely outcome, but it is nonetheless possible. No one is in a position at this point to predict the level of discoveries either in the continental shelf or in the western basins. If I were a Chinese planner, I would count on an oil and gas industry on the order of the lower sets of curves, R_1 and R_2.

We are now in a position to assess more generally the balance between the production and consumption sectors of the Chinese energy economy (see Figure 6.4). These curves represent a variety of resource and economic growth assumptions. The solid lines represent energy availability from domestic production; the dashed lines represent aggregate consumption requirements. Note that the lines are paired in these three scenarios. The pairing of production and consumption occurs because of the feedback effect of rapid growth in energy production on general economic and industrial growth and thence back into energy consumption. This pairing would occur regardless of whether Beijing chooses a high export strategy or reserves the bulk of oil production for domestic consumption. The variation in consumption curves rests on tiny increments in the economic growth rate. The entire range of energy consumption curves represented here (S_1 to S_3) is produced by the difference between a 3.5 percent economic growth rate and a 5 percent annual rate of growth of oil production. Even under the most optimistic energy conservation scenarios, represented by low or decaying energy/GNP elasticities, a very small increment of additional economic growth produces large differences over time in energy consumption requirements. Thus, there is good reason to expect a feedback effect of large oil and gas resource discoveries on energy consumption, and the curves may therefore be reasonably paired. In reality, I believe that Chinese planners would have a difficult time with any attempts to decouple rapid growth in energy production from energy demand.

If these production and consumption curves represent anything like reality, they lead inexorably to two basic conclusions. The first is that

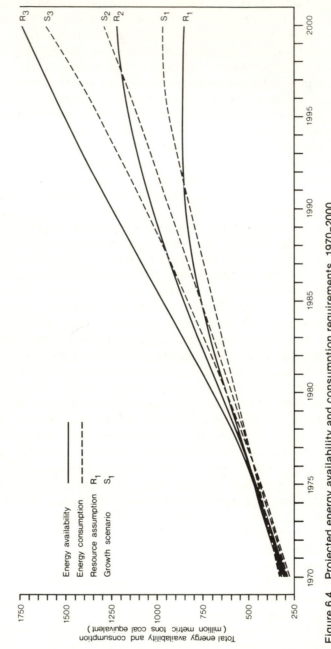

Figure 6.4   Projected energy availability and consumption requirements, 1970–2000

even under conditions of relatively limited oil and gas resource discoveries, China should, by the end of the century, approach the aggregate energy capability achieved by the Soviet energy system in the mid-1970s. Under extremely optimistic and not very likely assumptions, the Chinese energy system could approach the energy capabilities of the United States by the end of the century. This latter statement assumes, of course, that the United States is in a plateau phase in its own energy development and does not move onto a significantly higher plateau in the interim. Regardless of how one specifies this conclusion, it indicates that under a wide range of assumptions, the world should have at least three energy superpowers by the year 2000, not very far into the future as energy development goes.

The second major conclusion is confirmation of the widely held belief that China is not likely to be a large oil exporter. Notice that the vertical distance between the solid and dashed curves represents China's net energy export potential. Under the assumptions behind each pair of curves, the curves generate a long, thin lens or bubble of export potential. In each case, real exports must lie within the constraints described by the "export bubble." Beijing may choose to export less than the potential amount, but it cannot export more than the export ceiling without cutting directly into domestic economic growth by creating a domestic energy shortage.

Figure 6.5 illustrates essentially the same point. The solid curves represent net energy export potential under our three sets of resource and economic growth assumptions. Under the two lower and more likely scenarios, export potential would peak at between 50 and 75 million tons of oil equivalent, or 1 to 1.5 million barrels per day. Actual crude oil exports would most likely be between 0.5 and 0.8 million barrels per day, as part of the energy would be exported in the form of coal. Only under the bonanza resource-discovery scenario would China's crude oil exports become significant on the scale of the world market, and even then China would resemble Indonesia, not Saudi Arabia, as an oil exporter.

The basic point illustrated by these figures is that although China may be able to contribute somewhat to the petroleum market in Asia, the People's Republic should not be expected to become a world-class oil-exporting nation. Even the contribution to Asian energy markets would be peripheral, satisfying only a portion of Japan's voracious appetite for imported oil and doing little to alleviate the severe conditions faced by oil-importing developing countries throughout the

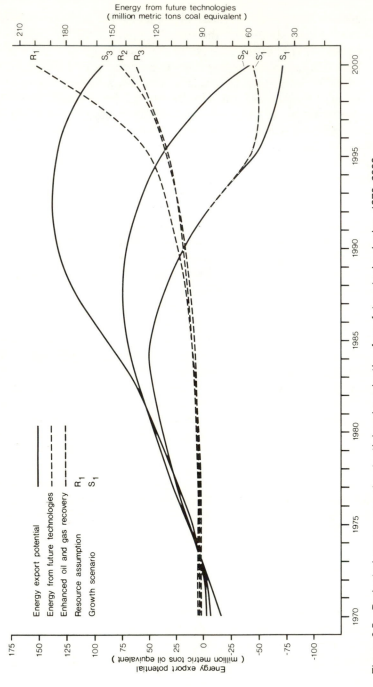

Figure 6.5 Projected energy export potential and production from future technologies, 1970–2000

region. China cannot be relied on within Asia to provide a sufficient quantity of oil exports to break through the development conditions imposed by the onset of the plateau phase of the world petroleum market. Asian developing countries must turn to the exploitation of their domestic energy resources – offshore gas, hydropower, geothermal, and other resources – to deal with the plateau phase. China is simply not in a position to help much, unless its oil and gas resources turn out to be much larger than expected.

What positive role can China play in the energy development of the Asia-Pacific region, given the constraints on its oil export potential? I think there are a number of areas in which Beijing can play an active energy role in the region, including the following:

1. Intermediate-level Chinese energy production technology may be highly appropriate to the development needs of other countries in the region and should be shared through trade and through Chinese technical assistance programs.
2. Beijing should actively seek to share Chinese experience in rural energy development. China is well ahead of other countries in the region in the development of appropriate energy technologies for the rural areas, such as the use of biogas generators and the installation of small-scale hydropower stations for rural electrification.
3. China should be active in cooperative information exchange programs directed toward the energy development of the region as a whole.
4. Beijing should seek to maximize the stabilizing effect of its regional oil and coal exports, however limited the ultimate scale of those exports.

A final word should be added about the link between regional energy cooperation and regional security relations. All my projections indicate that the People's Republic of China is moving toward the status of an energy superpower – roughly in the same class with the Soviet Union and the United States. There is little doubt that Beijing will make every effort to follow the precedent set by the superpowers in translating energy development into industrial power, and industrial power into strategic military capabilities. It would not, therefore, be surprising to find at least three major military powers, the United States, the Soviet Union, and China, in the world of the year 2000. This has profound implications for the global strategic balance and for global political relations.

China's newfound status as a superpower may have stabilizing or destabilizing effects in Asia and the Pacific, depending on the political evolution of the People's Republic itself. There is little the outside world can do to determine the course of that political evolution. But we can encourage China toward creative and stabilizing uses of its new strengths. One avenue for providing this necessary encouragement is to gradually incorporate the People's Republic into regional security coalitions. This means that the United States should strengthen the tacit security coalition among China, Japan, and the United States. It also means that we should encourage expanded political contacts between China and the ASEAN community. We are well on the way toward ending China's isolation in the Asia-Pacific region and in the international community. Further steps should be taken to strengthen our energy cooperation with China, and ultimately our cooperation on deeper political and security issues. This process must take place in a slow and evolutionary manner, without risking the freedom or independence of the countries around China's perimeter. But the process should continue at a steady pace now, in the early 1980s, to ensure a stable, integrated, and secure relationship with China as it emerges into a position of world power.

Bibliography

Cheng, Chu-yuan. *China's Petroleum Industry: Output Growth and Export Potential.* New York: Praeger Publishers, 1976.

Hardy, Randall W. *China's Oil Future: A Case of Modest Expectations.* Boulder, Colo.: Westview Press, 1978.

Harrison, Selig S. *China, Oil, and Asia: Conflict Ahead?* New York: Columbia University Press, 1977.

Ling, H. C. *The Petroleum Industry of the People's Republic of China.* Stanford, Calif.: Hoover Institution Press, 1975.

Meyerhoff, A. A., and J. O. Willums. "Petroleum Geology and Industry of the People's Republic of China." *CCOP Technical Bulletin* (United Nations Economic and Social Council for Asia and the Pacific) 10 (December 1976):103–104.

Smil, Vaclav. *China's Energy: Achievements, Problems, Prospects.* New York: Praeger Publishers, 1976.

Smil, Vaclav, and Kim Woodard. "Perspectives on Energy in the People's Republic of China." *Annual Review of Energy* 2 (1977):307–341.

Woodard, Kim. "China's Energy Development in Global Perspective." In James C. Hsiung and Samuel S. Kim, eds., *China in the Global Community.* New York: Praeger Publishers, 1980, pp. 120–139.

Woodard, Kim. *The International Energy Relations of China* (Stanford, Calif.: Stanford University Press, 1980) 717 pp.

Woodard, Kim. "The Second Transition: America in Asia under Carter." *SAIS Review* 1 (Winter 1981):129–148.

Wu, Yuan-li, and H. C. Ling. *Economic Development and the Use of Energy Resources in Communist China.* New York: Praeger Publishers, 1963.

7210
6323
China

7

China's Maritime Jurisdictions: The Future of Offshore Oil and Fishing

Choon-ho Park

China has a coastline of approximately 11,000 kilometers and, when some 3,500 islands in its coastal and offshore waters are included, another 10,000 kilometers can be added to this figure.[1] The length of the coastline alone indicates the importance of the sea for China. Unlike the early modern maritime powers of the West, such as Spain, the Netherlands, and Great Britain, however, the Middle Kingdom did not use the sea intensely. Basically a land power, China's interest in the sea was limited to defense and fishing and other economic purposes. The Chinese regarded the sea as a natural defense against attacks by barbarians until the mid-nineteenth century, when the sea became a convenient route for foreign invaders. In each of the six major invasions China sustained between 1842 and 1900, the sea was in fact the enemies' route of entry, and on three of the six occasions, Bohai Bay was used to reach Beijing, less than a hundred miles inland. On the economic side, China's maritime trade was confined to meeting the marginal needs of a self-contained continental economy. In this regard, Ching Emperor Chienlung's response to King George III's McCartney trade mission to China in 1793 may be noted with interest.

> As your Ambassador can see for himself, we possess all things. I set no value on objects strange or ingenious, and have no use for your country's manufactures. . . . I do not forget the lonely remoteness of your island, cut off from the world by intervening wastes of sea, nor do I overlook your excusable ignorance of the usages of Our Celestial Empire.[2]

Specifically with respect to marine resources, therefore, not until the mid-1950s did China feel the need to assert its maritime jurisdiction, and then the initial concern was over regulation of foreign – mainly Japanese – fishing in China's offshore waters of the Yellow and East China seas. As will be described in the last section of this chapter, the People's Republic concluded an informal fisheries arrangement with Japan in 1955. The Japanese had pressed for such an agreement because they wanted to stop Chinese seizure of Japanese fishing vessels on allegations of espionage or other unacceptable charges. On the occasion of these fishing negotiations, Japan, to its great surprise, learned that China had three maritime security zones, which had been in effect since 1950. In China's view, entry of foreign vessels into the zones was possible only with prior consent or at their own risk.[3]

Of basic importance to the maritime jurisdiction of a coastal state is the breadth of its territorial sea. The People's Republic declared a territorial sea limit of up to 12 nautical miles for the first time in September 1958.[4] This declaration roughly followed the formula of the Convention on the Territorial Sea and the Contiguous Zone, signed in Geneva in April of that year. The timing of the declaration was not arbitrary but was in response to the report that in the late summer of 1958 Taiwan, with U.S. support, had reinforced its defense of Quemoy and Matsu, two offshore islands under Taiwan's control but well within 12 miles of the mainland.[5]

At the end of the 1960s and the beginning of the 1970s, China and other coastal states started to lay claim to the continental shelf resources – oil, primarily – of the semienclosed seas of Northeast Asia. China was among the first – as early as the late 1950s[6] – to hint that there might be oil in some parts of the Yellow and East China seas. Because marine geologists were pessimistic about finding oil in the waters of this region, however, no active exploration was undertaken until the late 1960s, when favorable reports began to arouse interest in the area and new offshore-oil development technology was becoming available. The combination of these factors led in 1966 to the formation of a joint exploration effort, under UN sponsorship, to conduct a geophysical survey in the Yellow and East China seas late in 1968.[7]

The oft-quoted survey was made public early in 1969 and caused a great sensation among coastal states that have debilitating shortages of oil. According to one of the conclusions of the report, "a high probability exists that the continental shelf between Taiwan and Japan may be one of the most prolific oil reservoirs in the world."[8] Although serious observers feared this statement was a gross exaggeration, it set off an instant "seabed oil war" in Northeast Asia, as the coastal states rushed into a "seagrab" competition. As a result, Japan, South Korea, and Taiwan staked out seventeen seabed oil zones in the Yellow and East China seas, thirteen of them overlapping one another. Furthermore, those three coastal states had signed oil concession contracts for most of their respective seabed zones with Western oil companies by the end of September 1970.[9]

Each of the three claimants adhered to its own unilateral claims, and the whole controversy became tightly locked in an endless legal scramble. Each claimant, taking advantage of the fact that the provisions of international law regarding delimitation of continental shelf boundaries were not specific enough to be readily applicable to their situation, interpreted the delimitation criteria to its own advantage. In search of a way out of this deadlock, they hit on the seemingly practical idea of a joint development scheme: They would put the boundary issues aside for future negotiation and proceed to develop the oil resources jointly. By the end of 1970, preparations had been made to form a joint oil-development committee consisting of private oil interests from the three coastal states.

It was at this juncture, in December 1970, that China, which had previously been silent, came forward with a strong protest.[10] China did not specify its own claims but simply asserted its "sovereign rights" to the continental shelf of the Yellow and East China seas. Japan, South Korea, and Taiwan, as well as the United States, whose oil companies were involved in the troubled waters, were so sensitive to the Chinese protest that the first attempt at joint development was abandoned even before its merits could be put to the test (a second attempt has since been made, as will be noted later). The Chinese intervention, as well as a North Korean protest alleging the South Korean claims to be illegal, has made the seabed controversy a five-party dispute, which has been further complicated by the ambiguity of the law of the sea and the territorial disputes that have incidentally arisen among some of the claimants (these will be discussed later).

Legal Aspects of the Seabed
Controversy in the China Seas

With respect to seabed jurisdiction, each coastal state of the Yellow and East China seas has sought to apply the particular criterion of international law that is most advantageous to its own interests. Japan has insisted on the median-line principle, China and Taiwan on the principle of the natural prolongation of land territory, and South Korea on a hybrid, that is, the median-line principle vis-à-vis China in the Yellow Sea and the principle of the prolongation of land territory vis-à-vis Japan in the East China Sea. The median-line principle derives from the Geneva Convention on the Territorial Sea and the Contiguous Zone of 1958, and the principle of natural prolongation of land territory from the judgment of the International Court of Justice on the North Sea Continental Shelf Cases of 1969. This new criterion has substantially undermined the universality of the median-line principle, and the seabed topography of the Yellow and East China seas would appear to enhance the positions of China and South Korea in relation to that of Japan, should the principle of the natural prolongation of land territory be rigidly applied to their situation.

The emergence of the exclusive 200-mile economic zone in 1972, which is certain to be accepted in the forthcoming new law of the sea, has in turn weakened the applicability of the principle of the natural prolongation of land territory, because in waters less than 400 miles wide, such as the Yellow and East China seas, the depth of the sea would cease to be a factor in boundary delimitation. This is a turn of events advantageous to Japan. If the law itself evolves in the middle of the controversy, it would be difficult for the coastal states to agree on any particular principle. It appears doubtful that the controversy will be settled solely as a legal issue, however, because, to the parties involved, anything affecting their oil interests would indeed be too important to be left to considerations of international law alone.

Similar situations exist, to different degrees of complexity, in the northern part of the Yellow Sea between China and North Korea, in the Gulf of Tonkin between China and Vietnam, and in the South China Sea among China and other coastal states. Most of the coastal states thus find their claims interlocked with those of others.[11] The current UN Law of the Sea Conference is expected to conclude its eight-year deliberations sometime late in 1982 (as scheduled); the coastal states of the China seas will have to review the old issues in light of the criteria to be embodied in the new law of the sea.

Current Oil Development Activities

In most parts of the Yellow and East China seas, the intransigent attitude of the coastal states toward sea-boundary delimitation has discouraged further involvement by foreign oil companies. Oil development activities are under way, therefore, only in areas close to the coast where the jurisdiction of the coastal state is not contested. In a disputed area of the East China Sea, however, an exception does exist. In Japan and South Korea, the fascination with joint development persisted despite the failure of the first attempt. In January 1974, they signed an agreement, disregarding the Chinese objection; the agreement came into force in June 1978, enabling the two countries to resume oil exploration in areas that in their view lie beyond Chinese jurisdiction.[12] As China regards the joint endeavor as an encroachment on its sovereign rights, the situation can be said to be volatile.

Since May 1978 China has signed a series of contracts with fifty-seven Western oil companies to conduct seismic surveys in eight designated areas of the South China Sea, the southern part of the Yellow Sea, and Bohai Bay.[13] Reportedly, most of the surveys were completed early in July 1980, and the foreign participants will now be invited to tender bids, so that oil exploration could begin between the end of 1980 and the first half of 1981. Another report suggests that two French oil companies, CFP and Elf/Aquitaine, were the first to sign oil exploration and production contracts with China, the risksharing arrangements having been initialed at the end of April 1980.[14]

China has been conducting its own exploration under the auspices of its Ministry of Geology and its National Oil and Gas Exploration Corporation. Hong Kong's *Shinwanbao* [New Evening News] reported in July 1980 a second discovery of oil about 100 nautical miles off Hong Kong in the South China Sea, after the first discovery at the estuary of the Pearl River in August 1979.[15]

Territorial Disputes over Offshore Islands[16]

Problems of maritime jurisdiction in the China seas have been greatly complicated by the presence of numerous islands in the East and South China seas whose ownership is contested by different claimants. In the East China Sea, eight uninhabited islands (Diaoyutai in Chinese and Senkaku in Japanese) situated northeast of Taiwan and west of Okinawa were claimed first by both Japan and Taiwan and now by China as well. The dispute arose in July 1970, when Taiwan made it clear that it considered the islands to be in its seabed zone in order to conduct oil exploration with Gulf Oil, thereby inviting strong protest from Japan, which asserted Japanese ownership. In the South China Sea, the territorial issues are far more complicated because the four archipelagos, including the submerged Macclesfield Bank, are claimed in whole or in part by China, Malaysia, the Philippines, Taiwan, and Vietnam. Each of these last three claimants is in control of some of the islands, and the Philippines is reported to have found oil in the disputed Reed Bank area.

Unless the disputants try to develop jointly the oil in the areas in question, following the example of Japan and South Korea, development of oil in the troubled waters will be delayed until the territorial issues are settled. But territories in East Asia have seldom changed hands peacefully and, partly for this historical reason, territorial issues easily fire the national sentiments of the peoples involved. Each claimant is also motivated by the potential seabed resources to which ownership of the "flyspecks" may entitle it. In a region without a tradition of settling disputes among nations by adjudication or other forms of third-party involvement, these factors may make negotiated settlement of such issues an impossibly difficult undertaking.

Fishing Right Problems

China has fertile fishing grounds in the semienclosed seas around its territory. The number of species in these seas is known to exceed 1,500 altogether, of which some 250 are found in the Yellow Sea and another 400 in the East China Sea. Coastal and offshore fishing in China, however, concentrate mainly on some 50 species, and a mere 4 yield a larger catch than the rest put together. The so-called "four major" fish are the small croaker, the large croaker, the girdlefish, and the white-scale herring. Of these, the two species of croakers alone contribute about 40 percent of the total annual catch.[17]

According to official figures, China caught 4.66 million tons of fish in 1978 and 4.31 million tons in 1979. These figures are significantly lower than earlier outside estimates, such as that by the UN Food and Agriculture Organization (FAO) of 6.88 million tons a year, but they still place China third in the world (after Japan and the Soviet Union) in terms of total annual catch.[18] In addition to its marine fishing, China is traditionally the leading freshwater fishing state, the total landing from its countless ponds, rivers, lakes, and rice paddies far exceeding 1 million tons and contributing more than 25 percent of the annual total quoted.

As I noted earlier, in 1955 China asserted its fishery jurisdiction in the Yellow and East China seas to regulate Japanese fishing there. The informal arrangements were subsequently incorporated into the formal fisheries agreement of 1975, which still remains in force. In the northern part of the Yellow Sea, interfishing between Chinese and North Korean fishermen is known to be regulated by agreement, although the details are not readily available to outside observers. Nor is information on Chinese and Vietnamese fishing in the Gulf of Tonkin available. No bilateral or multilateral fisheries arrangements are known to exist between China and other coastal states of the South China Sea.

The Chinese government has occasionally made efforts to promote the fishing industry by means of long-term planning, first as part of the National Program for Agricultural Development of 1956–1967 and most recently as a separate plan for 1976–1985.[19] In each case, it is interesting that the emphasis has shifted from shallow-water fishing to deep-water fishing, whereas in other countries planning is usually based on a variety of factors, including the distance from the coast to the coastal, offshore, and distant-water fishing grounds and vessel tonnage. This may be an indication that China has yet to build up a distant-water fishing industry comparable to those of other developing countries like South Korea.

Since October 1972, when it replaced Taiwan at the United Nations, the People's Republic has been most active in its support of the 200-mile limit. This activity has naturally raised the expectation of outside observers that China itself would adopt the 200-mile limit in due course. But with even Singapore's deciding in mid-September 1980 to join the "200-milers," China is now one of only two coastal states of the region (the other is South Korea) not to have declared a 200-mile fishing or economic zone. As China's semienclosed seas are nowhere as wide as 400 miles from one headland or island to another, it would appear that alternative arrangements such as the one with Japan would do just as well, especially since a 200-mile limit would only create more boundary disputes.

Summary Observations

In 1979, China's crude oil production increased only 2 percent over the previous year. Official sources also admitted in September 1980 that the 1978 estimates of future crude oil production were unrealistically high and that actual output would level off at best or even decline in subsequent plan years. Crude oil exports to Japan would also have to be reduced from the original pledges of 9.5 million tons in 1981 and 15 million tons in 1982.[20] Although these shortfalls would probably make China more eager to develop its offshore oil reserves, there would nevertheless be no need to assume a more compromising attitude in relation to sea boundary problems with its opposite or adjacent neighbors; the areas being explored are so close to its coast that jurisdiction could not be contested by other coastal states. Consequently, China's maritime boundary problems with its neighbors are likely to remain unresolved in the foreseeable future.

China is still under no pressure to declare a 200-mile limit, and if it chooses to follow the fashion of the times, the baselines from which the distance could be measured would be made unspecific, as in the 1958 declaration of territorial waters.

With respect to its possible interest in distant-water fishing, China must know that most of the world's major fishing grounds have now fallen under national jurisdiction: Distant-water fishing is no longer as economically attractive as it was prior to 1977, when the "200-mile" age began.

Notes

1. Choon-ho Park, "Fishing Under Troubled Waters: The Northeast Asia Fisheries Controversy," *Ocean Development and International Law* 2:2 (1974): 94.

2. Richard L. Walker, ed., "China and the West: Cultural Collision, Selected Documents," Yale University, Far Eastern Studies Program (mimeographed), 1956, pp. 28–29.

3. Park, "Fishing," pp. 110–122.

4. UN Document A/34/712:S/13640, November 23, 1979, p. 10 (reprinted version with new transcription).

5. Jerome Cohen and Hungdah Chiu, *People's China and International Law*, 2 vols. (Princeton, N.J.: Princeton University Press, 1974), vol. 1, p. 469.

6. S. C. Fan and Y.S. Chu, "Zhongguo Donghai he Huanghai Nanbu Dizhidi Chubu Yenjiu" [Preliminary study of submarine geology of China's East Sea and the southern Yellow Sea], *Haiyang yu Huzhao* [Oceanologia et Limnologia], 2 (April 1959): 82–85.

7. Choon-Ho Park, "Oil Under Troubled Waters: The Northeast Asia Sea-Bed Controversy," *Harvard International Law Journal* 14:2 (Spring 1973): 212–213.

8. Ibid.

9. Ibid.

10. Ibid., pp. 229–234.

11. Choon-ho Park, "China and Maritime Jurisdiction: Some Boundary Issues," *German Yearbook of International Law* 22 (1979): 138.

12. Ibid., pp. 130–137.

13. *Foreign Broadcast Information Service*, vol. 1, China, July 21, 1980, p. A1; and Kevin Fountain, "The Development of China's Offshore Oil," *China Business Review* (January-February 1980): 33.

14. *London Oil Reports*, May 12, 1980, p. 3.

15. *Shinwanbao* [New Evening News], July 25, 1980 (AP and DJ: Hong Kong).

16. Park, "China and Maritime Jurisdiction," pp. 126–130.

17. Park, "Fishing," p. 96. Also see *Nanhai Zhudao Haiyu Yuleizhi* [The fishes

of the islands in the South China Sea] (Beijing: Science Press, 1979), p. iii.

18. Jaydee Hanson, "China's Fisheries: Scaling Up Production," *China Business Review* (May-June 1980): 25.

19. Park, "Fishing," p. 128; and Hanson, "China's Fisheries," p. 26.

20. *Asahi Shinbun*, September 12, 1980, morning ed., p. 1.

N A

8

Southeast Asia Looks at China

Guy J. Pauker

The historical process shaping power relations among states in the Asia-Pacific region was controlled for three decades by U.S. military superiority and by the willingness of the American people to oppose the expansion of Soviet power. After the collapse in April 1975 of U.S. efforts to implement in Indochina a policy of containment aimed at preventing communist expansion beyond the boundaries established at the end of World War II, a new geopolitical situation began to emerge.

After April 1975, the United States, which had never before lost a war, retrenched militarily, rejecting the role of "global policeman"—this at a time when Soviet efforts to achieve global power status were just beginning to yield returns. At the end of 1978, less than four years after the U.S. withdrawal, these changes in the balance of political-military forces between the two superpowers had manifested themselves in the Asia-Pacific region. Soviet military operations in Afghanistan, the occupation of Cambodia by Vietnamese troops supported logistically by the Soviet Union, and the presence of elements of the Soviet Pacific Fleet and Pacific Air Force at the former U.S. Camranh Bay and Danang bases all indicated that the global order established at the end of World War II was crumbling.

Among the noncommunist nations of Southeast Asia, as well as in other countries, these developments aroused anxiety and caused uncertainty about the conduct of international relations as the threats to their national existence became more complex and difficult to manage. Weakened confidence in U.S. willingness and capacity to play a stabilizing role in the Asia-Pacific region and concern about Soviet intentions prompted the five countries of the Association of Southeast Asian Nations (ASEAN) to take a more active and vocal role in defense of their national and regional interests than in the past. At the United Nations and in the daily conduct of their international relations, these nations—Indonesia, Malaysia, the Philippines, Singapore, and Thailand—adopted a firm position against foreign intervention in the domestic affairs of any country, refusing to recognize the Heng Samrin government established by Vietnamese troops in Phnom Penh and denouncing Soviet military operations in Afghanistan.

In pursuit of this policy, the ASEAN governments found themselves following paths parallel to those of China and the United States—two former enemies who were drawn closer together by the realization that neither was in a position to block independently the growing expansionist tendencies of the Soviet Union. But whereas the opposition of the United States and China to Soviet hegemony in Asia, which they first proclaimed jointly in the Shanghai Communique of 1972, has been relatively straightforward, the ASEAN governments face major dilemmas in deciding for the short and long run how to cope with what they perceive to be the primary threat to their national interests.

The five ASEAN governments all have ample experience with communist subversion and insurgency; they are suspicious of the Soviet Union and view it as the fountainhead, at least in the past, of world revolution. The ASEAN nations, which are relatively weak and have been the helpless victims of the superior military capabilities of external powers, view with concern the growing Soviet deployment of forces in their region. Yet their historical experience does not include significant specific episodes of military coercion, political dominance, or economic exploitation by the Soviet Union, which is furthermore geographically remote and therefore perceived as less of a threat than other major powers that evoke vivid historical memories of interference in the region: the European powers, which dominated during long centuries of colonialism; Japan, whose brutal military occupation from 1941 to 1945 is still remembered; the United States, still associated with its conquest of the Philippines and the war waged in Indochina; and last but not least, China.

Fear of China has deep historical roots in Southeast Asia. In the Chinese world order, neighboring rulers were viewed as "local authorities," who had to be subordinated to the central and awe-inspiring power of the emperor. The extent of Chinese control was limited only by China's capacity to enforce its authority over outlying areas, primarily through the tributary system, not by rules of international law governing relations among independent, sovereign states. After the Chinese Communist Party seized full control of the mainland in 1949, fear of revolutionary subversion was added to the traditional concerns of Southeast Asia's ruling elites about their giant neighbor. They now saw not only their national identities but also their class interests threatened by China, which was training, arming, and guiding communist parties in the countries of Southeast Asia and giving them vocal propagandistic support through all the media available.

From U.S. perspective, China is now in the process of radically changing its domestic and international policies, driven by the desire to modernize the economy and by the fear of Soviet enmity and encirclement. But from a Southeast Asian perspective, China still poses a number of distinct though interrelated threats, which are not necessarily diminishing as a result of the increasing, close economic collaboration with Japan and the United States and the emergence of a common front among these three powers against the Soviet Union.

Of particular concern to the ASEAN countries, as well as to the other neighbors of China in southern Asia, are the following factors:

1. China's one billion very poor people, living in a backward country, are seen as a demographic threat to Southeast Asia, whose fertile lands and natural resources could become increasingly attractive to the hard-working and dynamic Chinese. What form that threat would take, if it were to materialize, is not clear to the governments of Southeast Asia. Although territorial conquest is outlawed by the charter of the United Nations, the establishment of puppet governments by the Soviet Union and by Vietnam provides disturbing precedents. More ominous yet, the millions of illegal immigrants, "boat people," and other refugees demonstrate that traditional methods of migration control are obsolete and that even strong countries can be invaded by large numbers of spontaneous or forced migrants. These problems have no easy remedies that are compatible with contemporary standards of human rights.

2. Under the discipline of a strong government, a resurgent China is likely to assert its geopolitical influence in the region under any circumstances, but especially in the setting of the Sino-Soviet rivalry, with obvious implications for the freedom of its neighbors. In this respect, China's sustained logistic and political support of the Khmer Rouge regime in Cambodia, following the Vietnamese invasion of December 1978, and the destructive border campaign of February 1979, aimed at "teaching a lesson" to the Vietnamese, are seen by the rest of Southeast Asia as ominous portents of things to come, even if in the short run Chinese actions were viewed as useful means for the containment of Vietnamese expansionism.

3. Extensive territorial claims in the South China Sea are potential

sources of conflict between China and Vietnam, Malaysia, and the Philippines. An ominous precedent was set in January 1974, when Chinese forces attacked and captured the South Vietnamese garrison stationed on the Paracel Islands. Since the establishment of the Socialist Republic of Vietnam, Hanoi's claim to the Paracels has been consistently rejected by Beijing. In June 1976, China asserted "indisputable sovereignty" over the Spratly Archipelago, which is also claimed primarily by the Philippines, but by Taiwan and Vietnam as well.

Although China has not actively pursued that claim against the Philippines, the border wars with India in 1962 and with Vietnam in 1979 were proof that China does not hesitate to use force in pursuit of its national interests. Long articles in the Chinese press keep reminding Southeast Asia that China's territorial claims in the South China Sea must be taken seriously. For instance, on April 7, 1980, the *People's Daily* responded to a Vietnamese Foreign Ministry white paper entitled "Vietnamese Sovereignty over the Huang Sa and Truong Sa Archipelagoes" with a lengthy article titled "The Xisha [Paracel] and Nansha [Spratly] Islands Have Been Chinese Territory Since Ancient Times." Several other articles in various Chinese publications have elaborated the archaeological, historical, and legal evidence invoked by the Chinese authorities in support of their territorial claims in the South China Sea. Although their arguments are aimed at Vietnam, they also challenge by implication the interests of all other littoral states in the South China Sea.

4. About 19 million overseas Chinese live in Southeast Asia as the result of spontaneous migration going back many centuries. The policy of the Chinese government with regard to these people has been ambiguous. The Australian scholar Stephen Fitzgerald, former ambassador to Beijing, pointed out in his 1972 book *China and the Overseas Chinese* that the Chinese residents of Southeast Asia can be viewed either as individual immigrants who became free as the countries in which they lived achieved independence, or as colonial communities of China, exploiting the local population and sending remittances to their relatives back home.

Since about 1954, when Chinese leaders attempted to improve relations with the "bourgeois nationalist" governments of Southeast Asia, the CCP has appealed to overseas Chinese to transfer their allegiance to their countries of residence and assimilate. It also decided to abandon the principle of dual nationality in order to facilitate relations with the countries of Southeast Asia. But the implementation of that policy has been difficult because of strong anti-Chinese feelings in the countries of Southeast Asia.

Although it has encouraged their assimilation, the CCP has also reacted vigorously in a number of instances in defense of overseas Chinese persecuted in Southeast Asia. In May 1978, following the exodus of some 200,000 Chinese from Vietnam to China, a new Overseas Chinese Affairs Office was established in Beijing, headed by Liao Chengzhi. Liao had been in charge of Chinese Overseas Affairs from 1949 until 1967, when he came under strong radical attack during the Cultural Revolution for "strangling and ruining the culture and education of overseas Chinese" and his office was abolished.

5. Last but not least, although Chinese leaders have repeatedly proclaimed that "revolution cannot be exported," the CCP maintains ties with communist parties in Southeast Asia that are committed to the overthrow of the national governments of their respective countries by subversion and armed struggle. In curious contrast with the pragmatic main line of Chinese foreign and domestic policies currently pursued under the leadership of Deng Xiaoping, China is still making available propaganda facilities to the clandestine communist parties of Southeast Asia. A striking example was the fiftieth anniversary of the Communist Party of Malaya (CPM), on April 30, 1980. The "Voice of the Malay Revolution," broadcasting from Yunnan in southern China, carried lengthy congratulatory messages from the communist parties of Burma, the Philippines, Indonesia, and Thailand, as well as an extensive statement by the leaders of the CPM. All parties pledged allegiance to "Mao Zedong Thought," on which the Chinese Communist Party itself now appears at best lukewarm. They also pledged to overthrow by armed struggle the governments of their respective countries. It would seem that the Chinese leadership is unwilling to terminate clandestine party-to-party relations for the sake of better government-to-government ties with the countries of Southeast Asia.

The anniversary of the CPM was not a unique instance. In late May 1980, the "Voice of the Malay Revolution" broadcast a lengthy statement signed by Yusuf Ajitorop, a member of the Politburo of the Communist Party of Indonesia (PKI) who has lived in China since the Indonesian upheaval of September 1965. In connection with the sixtieth anniversary of the PKI, he vehemently attacked the Suharto government and warned that "it would be a grave mistake and dangerous to regard Vietnam, which has ambitions of regional hegemonism, supported by the Soviet Union, as a buffer zone against the so-called Chinese 'Threat from the North.'" Naturally, that broadcast was as offensive to the Indonesian government as the congratulatory messages to the CPM had been to the Malaysian government a month earlier.

The Chinese Communist Party may have used these broadcasts to warn Indonesia and Malaysia against a policy of reconciliation with Vietnam. In sharp contrast with these provocative broadcasts, another clandestine radio station in southern China, the "Voice of the People of Thailand," had gone off the air in July 1979 as an obvious reward to the Thai military government for supporting China's policy of armed resistance, through the Khmer Rouge guerrillas of Pol Pot, against the Vietnamese troops in Cambodia and the Heng Samrin government in Phnom Penh. The CCP has apparently ceased whatever support it had previously given to the Communist Party of Thailand (CPT) and to the Burmese Communist Party (BCP). According to Burmese government officials, the BCP has recently become deeply involved in the opium trade to compensate for the loss of Chinese support after 1978 while it engages the Burmese army in heavy combat in defense of communist base areas.

China confronts the governments of Southeast Asia with difficult policy choices. Before the proclamation of the Nixon Doctrine in 1969, the United States was viewed in Southeast Asia as the protector of noncommunist regimes against Chinese subversion or expansionism. Soviet-American geopolitical competition gradually prompted the United States to abandon the policy of containment of China, which in turn was seeking support against the Soviet Union. The logic of the situation dictated a new power alignment. But the possibility of a Sino-Japanese-American anti-Soviet coalition is a disturbing prospect for Indonesia and Malaysia, which fear China more than they fear the Soviet Union. All present ASEAN governments seem to prefer a continued U.S. presence in the region to either Soviet or Chinese dominance, but they do not necessarily prefer China to the U.S.S.R. From a Southeast Asian perspective, U.S. disengagement is viewed as creating a power vacuum in the region that could set the stage for an increasingly ominous Sino-Soviet competition.

Some circles even fear, as a "worst case" assumption, that playing the "China card" might prompt the United States to give support to Chinese hegemonial aspirations in Southeast Asia as a substitute for the security role U.S. forces had played in the region in the past. In those circles it is argued privately that such a development would constitute a greater threat to the national interests of the ASEAN nations than a Soviet presence based on the 1978 alliance with Vietnam. These fears were in part reflected in early 1980 in the diplomatic maneuvers of Indonesia and Malaysia, which were seeking to open a dialogue with Vietnam. Temporarily at least, these long-range considerations had to give way to the more urgent need to assert ASEAN solidarity after the invasion by Vietnamese troops of some Thai border areas in June 1980.

China's erratic foreign policy record since 1949 raises serious doubts in Southeast Asian governments about their future relations with the government in Beijing. Periods of communist and chauvinist Chinese militancy have alternated with periods of "peaceful coexistence"; such changes are complexly correlated with domestic political developments in China. At present, the conflict with the Soviet Union and Vietnam and the need for external assistance in support of the Four Modernizations movement is prompting China to improve its image in the West and in Japan by bettering its relations with the ASEAN countries, as it had done once before, during the 1954–1959 "Bandung Period." Neither the record of the last three decades nor some recent official statements are reassuring to the governments of Southeast Asia, which believe that China could again switch to a militant policy of confrontation if the ASEAN nations failed to live up to its expectations, especially in their policies toward the Soviet Union.

In a revealing speech to a conference of Chinese diplomatic envoys held in Beijing in June 1979, Vice-Premier Ji Pengfei, director of the International Liaison Department of the CCP Central Committee, which is charged with maintaining contacts with "fraternal parties," explained that although such relations will not be cultivated through the channels of the Ministry of Foreign Affairs, they will be maintained through Party channels. He mentioned, as an example, that Thai communist leaders had held a conference in Beijing and had met with Chairman Hua, Vice-Chairman Deng and Vice-Chairman Ye, but the Chinese newspapers and radio stations were instructed not to report these meetings. Southeast Asian national security managers can hardly be reassured by such formalistic distinctions between government-to-government and party-to-party relations. Furthermore, they had been told explicitly by Deng Xiaoping during his visit to Southeast Asia in 1978 that the CCP would continue to support, on a party-to-party basis, communist organizations in Southeast Asia. They therefore assume, rightly or wrongly, that the CCP views the communist parties of Southeast Asia as potential weapons against their national governments if the latter become antagonistic to Chinese interests. Actually, the CCP may be unable to extend the present pragmatic policy of its new leaders to the sphere of party-to-party relations for fear that the parties that it abandons may shift their

allegiance to the Soviet-Vietnamese camp and facilitate the encirclement of China. One can argue that China stands to gain politically if
the local communist parties in Southeast Asia became pro-Soviet, as
this would deflect hostility and fear from Beijing to Moscow. But apparently the Chinese leaders do not see the situation this way.

In any event, the way the Chinese Communist Party applies political pressure seems rather heavyhanded and is probably counter-
productive. In support of revolutionary movements in Southeast Asia,
it has made clandestine radio stations in southern China available to
the Communist Party of Thailand since 1962, to Philippine Com-
munists since 1967, to the Communist Party of Malaysia since 1969,
and to the Communist Party of Burma since 1971. Radio Beijing has
also broadcast militant propaganda against various Southeast Asian
governments. The use of agitational broadcasts, either overtly by
Radio Beijing or covertly by stations made available to Southeast
Asian communist parties, is apparently directly related to current
events. If Thailand supports and assists China's policy in Cambodia,
both the clandestine "Voice of the People of Thailand" and Radio
Beijing cease broadcasting. But when the new Thai prime minister,
General Prem Tinsulanond, seemed to have second thoughts about
allowing China to supply the Khmer Rouge guerrillas, the Communist
party of Thailand was allowed to use the radio station of the Communist Party of Malaysia to attack the Prem government. As Malaysia
has not been fully responsive to Chinese policies, the clandestine
"Voice of the Malay Revolution" in Yunnan has continued its attacks
on the government in Kuala Lumpur, while Radio Beijing shifted last
year from attacks on the Malaysian government to silence and then,
more recently, to praise. Whether China derives political benefits
from such Pavlovian treatment of Southeast Asian governments is
open to question.

Despite a remarkable shift from ideology to pragmatism in its
economic policy and in some aspects of its foreign policy, China still
appears less than rational in its bitter conflict with Vietnam.
Regardless of whether Hanoi should have shown gratitude to Beijing
for past aid, which allegedly amounted to about $20 billion, neither
the punitive Chinese expedition against the Vietnamese borderlands
in February 1979 nor support of Pol Pot's guerrilla forces seems likely
to break the will of the Hanoi leadership. China's policy seems driven
more by vindictiveness than by cold geopolitical calculations. By using force against Vietnam and interfering in the internal affairs of
Cambodia, China is actually increasing Soviet leverage in Indochina.

Chinese failure to assuage the fears of Southeast Asian governments could eventually result in developments harmful to U.S. security interests in the Western Pacific. Unless ASEAN governments are convinced that they have no reason to fear China in the long run, some influential Southeast Asian circles might be prompted to tolerate or even encourage an increased Soviet role in the region as a countervailing force against possible future Chinese dominance. Pro-Soviet propensities would obviously be enhanced if the ASEAN governments concluded that the United States is indifferent to the fate of Southeast Asia, lacks the capabilities and will to play a decisive role in the region, or even favors Chinese regional hegemony as part of an anti-Soviet global strategy.

China could make a unique contribution to the stability of Southeast Asian countries and to the welfare of their peoples by abandoning the disruptive activities of the Mao era and showing its neighbors that it is interested in the creation of a peaceful regional order. A constructive Chinese policy toward Southeast Asia would not seem more difficult to implement than the domestic changes initiated by Deng Xiaoping and his supporters since 1976. It is felt that such a policy in Southeast Asia should include four major elements: a humanitarian policy toward Cambodia; a new policy on party-to-party relations; resolution of the overseas Chinese issue; and settlement of offshore territorial claims in the South China Sea.

A Humanitarian Policy Toward Cambodia. Supporting the guerrilla forces of the abominable Pol Pot has not succeeded in coercing the Vietnamese into abandoning their puppet, Heng Samrin, but the protracted fighting is sacrificing helpless civilian survivors of war and genocide to abstract, cold-blooded geopolitical calculations. Although China cannot be expected to accept passively an aggressive Soviet-Vietnamese military alliance on its southern flank, the government of 1 billion Chinese should be able to find other ways to influence the policies of the government of 50 million Vietnamese than by the sacrifice of the remaining Khmer population.

A New Policy on Party-to-Party Relations. China has little to gain in the world and much to lose in Southeast Asia by continued support of the communist parties in the ASEAN countries and in Burma. Those terroristic and faction-ridden parties have for more than thirty years retarded the economic growth of the countries in which they operate by diverting governmental efforts and material resources from development to counterinsurgency, to the detriment primarily of the poorest elements of the population. China would be able to make a much stronger case that its modernization should be assisted by the industrial democracies if its party-to party policy in Southeast Asia did not hinder the modernization of its equally poor and deserving Southeast Asian neighbors.

Resolution of the Overseas Chinese Issue. The basic Chinese policy is constructive, encouraging overseas Chinese to assimilate. The government of the People's Republic, however, is willing to accept those who are forced to leave Southeast Asia or who want to return to the land of their ancestors. The overseas Chinese issue is fraught with emotions generated by economic envy and racial antagonism. These cannot be eliminated by decree, but the governments of Southeast Asia can create a legal and political framework facilitating the assimilation of overseas Chinese, as Indonesia is currently doing. China, in turn, has to be consistent in its policy toward people of Chinese ancestry. If it favors their assimilation, it should treat them the way it treats other foreigners–not an easy decision to make, as overseas Chinese are a major source of foreign exchange, making annual remittances to relatives in China in the range of US $500 million to $1 billion annually.

Settlement of Offshore Territorial Claims in the South China Sea. Assurances have apparently been conveyed to the Philippines that China will not use force in solving the dispute over the Spratly Archipelago. But no public declaration is on record comparable to the statement made by Deng Xiaoping on Japanese television in October 1978 concerning the dispute over the ownership of the Senkaku Islands in the East China Sea. Deng proposed that the issue be shelved, because "our generation does not have enough wisdom to solve this problem." With regard to the Paracel and Spratly islands, China's attitude is threatening to the other littoral countries around the South China Sea. That issue should also be left for future generations to solve, when the heat of current conflicts will have dissipated.

Unless China finds ways to clarify these major areas of concern to the countries of Southeast Asia and reassure her weaker neighbors, there will be no real improvement in their relationships. Indeed the situation will fester and may get even worse.

Selected Bibliography

Fitzgerald, Stephen. *China and the Overseas Chinese.* Cambridge: Cambridge University Press, 1972.
Martin, Edwin W. *Southeast Asia and China–The End of Containment.* Boulder, Colo.: Westview Press, 1977.

Pauker, Guy, et al. *Diversity and Development in Southeast Asia—The Coming Decade*. New York: McGraw-Hill, 1977.

Solomon, Richard H., ed. *Asian Security in the 1980s—Problems and Policies for a Time of Transition*. Cambridge, Mass.: Oelgeschlager, Gunn & Hain, Publishers, 1980.

Taylor, Jay. *China and Southeast Asia—Peking's Relations with Revolutionary Movements*. New York: Praeger Publishers, 1974.

The Contributors

A. Doak Barnett is senior fellow at the Brookings Institution. In 1976–1977, he was a fellow in the Communication Institute of the East-West Center.

Harrison Brown, director of the Resource Systems Institute of the East-West Center, is author of *The Human Future Revisited* (1978) and other books.

Godwin C. Chu is a research associate in the Communication Institute of the East-West Center. He is coeditor, with Francis L. K. Hsu, of *Moving a Mountain* (1979) and other books on the media and communication in modern China.

Francis L. K. Hsu, a fellow in the Communication Institute of the East-West Center, has been president of the American Anthropological Association. He is the author of *Americans and Chinese: Reflections on Two Cultures and Their People* (2d ed., 1970) and *Under the Ancestors' Shadow* (1971).

Choon-ho Park is a research associate in the Culture Learning Institute and the Environment and Policy Institute of the East-West Center.

Guy J. Pauker is a research associate in the Resource Systems Institute of the East-West Center.

Dwight H. Perkins is a professor of Modern China studies and professor of economics at Harvard University and a member of the Board of Governors of the East-West Center.

Chi-hsien Tuan is a research associate in the Population Institute of the East-West Center.

Allen S. Whiting is a member of the Department of Political Science and the Center for Chinese Studies at the University of Michigan.

Kim Woodard is a research associate in the Resource Systems Institute of the East-West Center.

Index

Afghanistan, Soviet invasion of,
    54, 115
Age structure. *See* Population
Agriculture, 7, 60
    as bottleneck, 6–8
    diversification, 62, 66
    experimental forms of, 24
    exports, 9
    and fertilizer use, 63
    grain imports, 59–60, 65–66
    grain production, 61
    ideological issues, 27, 30
    incentives, 22, 24, 61–62
    investment, 61
    irrigation, 8, 62–63
    mechanization of, 23, 63
    priority of, 60
    production, 44 n58, 62
    rice exports, 60
    rice yields, 7, 8, 63
    technicians, 64
    See also Food; Land
Amur River, management of, 52
Arable land. *See* Land
Argentina, grain exports, 60
ASEAN. *See* Association of
    Southeast Asian Nations
Asia-Pacific region
    China's role in, 102
    energy development in, 85, 101
    political alignment in, 87
    power relations within, 115
Association of Southeast Asian
    Nations (ASEAN), 87

and Communist insurgency, 116
concerns of, 117–120
contact with China, 102
international role, 115–116
pro-Soviet propensities, 123
Australia, grain exports, 60
Authority, abuse of, 28–30

Baikal-Amur Railroad (BAM),
    51–52, 53
Balance of payments, 86
BAM. *See* Baikal-Amur Railroad
Bangladesh, 12
Baochan daohu, 24–26
Baochan daozu (mutual aid teams),
    22
Barefoot doctors, 71
Basic accounting unit, 44–45 n60
BCP. *See* Communist Party of
    Burma
Birth control, 69
    economic incentives, 73
    quota system, 70
    See also Contraception;
        Population
Birthrate
    crude, 78(table)
    statistical reliability of, 77
Boat people, 117
Bolshevik revolution, 47
Border wars, 118
Bureaucratism, 39
    campaign against, 35
    rigidity of, 10, 29

Burmese Communist Party. *See*
    Communist Party of Burma
Burns, John A., x, 16

Cadres, 41 n1
    local reluctance to innovate,
        27–28
    reform of, 30–35
Cambodia
    occupation of, 115
    policy toward, 123
    See also Khmer Rouge
Canada, grain exports, 60
Capital formation, 10–11
Central Committee Documents
        (Zhongfa), 16–17, 22, 23,
        25, 30, 39
China and the Overseas Chinese
        (Fitzgerald), 118
China card, problems with, 3, 120
China Seas. *See* East China Sea;
    Yellow Sea
Chinese Communist Party, 116
    birth control role, 71
    Central Committee, 16–17, 32, 39
    International Liaison
        Department, 121
    isolationist groups within, 5–6
    party-to-party relations, 121, 123
    support of revolutionary
        movements, 122
Chinese Eastern Railroad, 47
Coal. *See* Energy
Coale, Ansley, 80–81
Collectivism, 26
Commission on Planned Birth, 70
Committee on the Present Danger,
    ix
Communes, 40 n1
    cadres in, 16, 29
    changes since 1976, 20–22
    communication linkages, 16–20
    exploitation within, 26
    original concept of, 61
    solidarity, 36–37

Communist Party of Burma (BCP),
    120
    radio stations, 122
Communist Party of Indonesia
    (PKI)
    politburo of, 119
Communist Party of Malaysia
    (CPM), 119
    radio stations, 122
Communist Party of Thailand
    (CPT), 120
    radio stations, 122
Communities, 40
Constitution of China (1978)
    and planned birth policy, 73
Continental shelf, 106–107
Contraception
    demand for, 70–71
    surgical, 71, 80
    usage rate, 79(table)
    See also Birth control;
        Population
CPM. *See* Communist Party of
    Malaysia
CPT. *See* Communist Party of
    Thailand
Crops. *See* Agriculture; Land
Cultural Revolution, 4, 25, 37, 38
    and agricultural extension
        services, 64
    disillusionment with, 5
    effects of, 1–2, 8

Da Gong Daily, 19
Deng Xiaoping, 4, 25, 119, 121,
    123
Dependency ratio. *See* Population

East China Sea
    fishing grounds, 110
    oil development in, 108–109
    unilateral claims to, 107
East-West Center, viii, xi
Economic growth
    constraints on, 6–11

implications of, 11–14
prospects for, 4–6
Economy, strengths of, 10–11
Education
emphasis in, ix
transnational, viii
Energy
balance projection model, 92–94
basic resources, 88
as bottleneck, 8–9
coal, 8, 88
development, 87, 89–90, 99
domestic system, 88–102
equipment imports, 91
export potential, 100(figure)
hydropower, 8, 88–89
natural gas, 54, 88, 96(figure)
noncommercial fuels, 91
nuclear power, 11
production technology, 90, 101
projections, 94–102
resource depletion dynamics,
95(figure)
and rural development, 101
in Third World, 85, 90
transportation fuels, 87
uranium, 89
See also Petroleum
Exploitation by landlords, 36, 37

Family
productive activities of, 20
target size, 75
FAO. *See* United Nations Food
and Agriculture Organization
Fertility. *See* Population
Feudalism, 29, 32
Fishing
arrangement with Japan, 106
promotion efforts, 111
rights problems, 110–111
Fitzgerald, Stephen *(China and the
Overseas Chinese)*, 118
Five Fixed Factors, Five
Coordinations, 23–24, 38

Food
global supplies, 59, 66, 67
malnutrition, 60
meat consumption, 65
requirements, 7, 64–65
See also Agriculture
Foreign exchange, as bottleneck,
9–10
Foreign policy, nature of, 121
Four Clean-Ups movement, 17
Four Modernizations campaign
ideal cadre for, 33
problems in, 18

Gandhi, Indira, 12
Gang of Four, 33
damage caused by, 30, 31, 33,
38
downfall of, 6, 15
purge of, 19, 31
radicalism of, 20, 30
Geneva Convention on the
Territorial Sea and the
Contiguous Zone of 1958, 108
GNP. *See* Gross national product
Grain. *See* Agriculture; Food
Great Leap Forward, 1, 4
Gross national product (GNP), 1
goals, 6
growth rate, 2, 11
Guangdong Code, 72–73
Gulf of Tonkin, 110
Gulf Oil Company, 109

Hong Kong, 109
Hua Guofeng, 29
Hu Yaobang, 4, 24
Hydropower. *See* Energy

IDA. *See* International
Development Association
IMF. *See* International Monetary
Fund
Income
distribution, 24

of peasants, 20, 25
  private, 21–22
India, view of China, 12
Indonesia, 12
  fear of China, 120
Industrialization, 1, 2, 101
Interdependence
  among nations, viii
  in Pacific region, xi
  risks of, 55
  and territorial disputes, 48
International Communications
    Agency, viii
International Development
    Association (IDA), 9
International Monetary Fund (IMF)
  China's membership in, 5, 9
International Rice Research
    Institute, 8
Iran, 86
Irrigation. See Agriculture
Islands, territorial disputes over,
    109–110

Japan, 54, 116
  economic success of, 3, 5
  energy consumption, 85
  as industrial giant, 1
  oil claims of, 107
  relations with Soviet Union,
    53–55
  Self-Defense Agency, 54
  and Siberian development, 53
  trade opportunities of, 12
Japanese Export-Import Bank,
    53, 55
Johnson, Lyndon B., x

Khmer Rouge, 120
  China's support of, 117, 122
  See also Cambodia
Khrushchev, Nikita, 52
Kleinjans, Everett, x
Korean peninsula, 56

Labor Force, 11
Land
  arable, 6, 62
  and hydropower development, 89
  in private plots, 15
  reform, 23, 37
  transactions with, 26
  See also Agriculture
Landlords, 39
  exploitation by, 37
Land Reform of 1950–1952,
    17–18
Law of the Sea, 108
Learn from Dazai movement, 17
  revamping of, 21
Liberation Army Daily, 19
Lieberthal, Kenneth, 16
Lin Biao, 17, 33
Liucun Commune. See Melon
    incident, Liucun Commune
Liu Shaoqi, 24, 38, 44 n58
Local autonomy
  degree of, 22–27
  restoration of, 21
  and stability, 37
Local solidarity, 35–38

Malaysia, 12
  fear of China, 120
Malnutrition. See Food
Manchuria, Japanese invasion of,
    47
Manufactures for export, 10
Mao Zedong, 4
  attack against Khrushchev, 49
  birth control policy, 82 n4
  stature of, 5
Maritime jurisdiction, 106
Mass media
  as communication channel, 16
  as conflict resolution mechanism,
    39–40
  credibility, 19
  since Gang of Four, 39
  role of, 18–20

Matsu, 106
Melon incident, Liucun Commune,
    28–30, 36, 37
Middle Kingdom, 105
Midwives, 71
Migration. *See* Population
Military
    capability, 101
    international competition, ix
    spending, 2–3
Ministry of Foreign Affairs, 121
Ministry of Geology, 109

National Oil and Gas Exploration
    Corporation, 109
National Program for Agricultural
    Development of 1956–1957,
    111
NATO. *See* North Atlantic Treaty
    Organization
Natural gas. *See* Energy
Nixon Doctrine of 1969, 120
North Atlantic Treaty Organization
    (NATO), 55
North Korea, 12
Nuclear conflict, viii
Nuclear power. *See* Energy

OPEC. *See* Organization of
    Petroleum Exporting Countries
Organization, systematic, 15–20
Organization of Petroleum
    Exporting Countries (OPEC),
    8, 86
Overseas Chinese issue, 118, 124

Pacific community, vision of, 48
Pakistan, 12
Paracel Islands, 118, 124
Pearl River, oil discovery in, 109
People's Commune movement, 24
People's Daily, 18, 20, 31
    and local concerns, 39
Petroleum
    exploration contracts, 8, 109

exports, 99–100, 111
    imports, 85
    production, 8, 96(figure), 111
    resources, 88
    world market, 86–87
Philippines
    Communist radio stations, 122
    view of China, 12
PKI. *See* Communist Party of
    Indonesia
Planned Birth Leadership Group,
    70
Planned Birth Office, 70
Political development, 13
Pol Pot, 48
Population
    age structure, 81
    aging coefficient, 75, 83 n18
    control of, 69
    dependency ratio, 75
    fertility rate, 72, 77, 80
    growth, 7, 60, 69
    migration control, 117
    100-year projection, 74(table)
    planned birth policy, 70–72,
        77–80
    single-child policy, 72–77
    U-shaped control, 75
    See also Birth control;
        Contraception
Port development, 53
Power, world balance of, 2
Production
    administration interference with,
        26
    central government quotas, 21
    private, 15–16, 21–22, 27, 28–30
Production brigades
    cadres in, 16
    lateral communication of, 39
Production team
    as basic unit, 15
    cadres in, 26
    during Gang of Four reign, 24
    lateral communication of, 39

plans, 28
and solidarity, 36
Propaganda, 119

Quemoy, 106

Radio Beijing, 122
Rice. *See* Agriculture
Rural communities, 15

Sakhalin, 53
Sea, as natural defense, 105
Seabed jurisdiction, 107
Second Marriage Law, 73–74
Security coalitions, 102
Security triangle, 87
Senkaku Islands
ownership issue, 48, 56, 124
Shanghai, 1
Siberia, 52
Singapore, 111
Single-child policy. *See* Population
Sino-American detente, 56
Sino-Japanese Treaty (1978), 54, 56
Sino-Soviet border
demarcation, 50
stability along, 11
Sino-Soviet relations, 11, 117
bilateral tensions, 49–51
and Siberian development, 51–53
trade, 56
Social fabric in rural China, 15,
38–40
South China Sea, 117–118, 124
Southeast Asia, fear of China,
12–13, 116
South Korea, 12
economic success of, 5
oil claims, 107
Soviet-Japanese relations, 53–55
Soviet Union
aid to China, 1, 11
economic growth, 3
education policy, ix
expansion, 87, 115

as grain importer, 59
in Indochina, 122, 123
invasion of Afghanistan, 54, 115
planning system, 10
post-Brezhnev leadership, 56–57
relationship with United States,
3
revisionism, 49
Spratly Islands, 118, 124
Stability, 123
dependence on growth, 6
Sun Yat-sen, 37
Superpower status, 3

Taiwan
China's threat to, 12
economic success of, 5
oil claims of, 107
Taiwan Strait, 56
Technology, 3
Territorial sea, 106
Textile industry, 9
Thailand, 120
China's threat to, 12
Third World, Sino-Soviet influence
in, 49
200-mile limit, 111–112

Union of Soviet Socialist Republics.
See Soviet Union
United Nations Food and
Agriculture Organization
(FAO), 110
United Nations Law of the Sea
Conference, 108
United States
China policy, 4, 13–14
food exports, 59
as imperialist power, ix
military superiority, 115
perspective on China, ix, 117
and Philippines conquest, 116
trade opportunities of, 13
Uranium. *See* Energy

Vietnam
  conflict with China, 48, 122
  Soviet alliance with, 120
  view of China, 12
  war with United States, 87
Village, role of, 36

Work teams, 17–18
World Bank, China's membership
  in, 5, 9
Wuding wutong. See Five Fixed
  Factors, Five Coordinations

Xinhua News Agency, 39, 42 n27

Yakutia, 54
Yalutsongpu River, 89
Yangze River, 7, 63
Yellow River, 7
Yellow Sea
  fishing grounds, 110
  oil development in, 108–109
  unilateral claims to, 107

Zhao Ziyang, 4, 24
Zhou Enlai, 4

THE EAST-WEST CENTER (Honolulu, Hawaii) is a national educational institution established in Hawaii by the U.S. Congress in 1960 to promote better relations and understanding between the United States and the nations of Asia and the Pacific through cooperative study, training, and research. Each year more than 1,500 men and women from the many nations and cultures work together in problem-oriented institutes or on "open" grants as they seek solutions to problems of mutual consequence to East and West. For each Center participant from the United States, two participants are sought from the Asian and Pacific area. The U.S. Congress provides basic funding for programs and a variety of awards to participants. Because of the cooperative nature of Center programs, financial support and cost-sharing are also provided by Asian and Pacific governments, regional agencies, private enterprise, and foundations. The Center is administered by a public, nonprofit corporation with an international Board of Governors.